Leaving Home

Other Books by Lynn Johnston

With This Ring
Family Business
Graduation: A Time for Change
The Big 5-0
Sunshine and Shadow
Middle Age Spread
Growing Like a Weed
Love Just Screws Everything Up
Starting from Scratch
"There Goes My Baby!"
Things Are Looking Up . . .
What, Me Pregnant?
If This Is a Lecture, How Long Will It Be?
Pushing 40
It's All Downhill from Here
Keep the Home Fries Burning
The Last Straw
Just One More Hug
"It Must Be Nice to Be Little"
Is This "One of Those Days," Daddy?
I've Got the One-More-Washload Blues . . .

Retrospectives

All About April
The Lives Behind the Lines: 20 Years of For Better or For Worse
Remembering Farley: A Tribute to the Life of Our Favorite Cartoon Dog
It's the Thought that Counts . . . Fifteenth Anniversary Collection
A Look Inside . . . For Better or For Worse: The 10th Anniversary Collection

Little Books

Isn't He Beautiful?
Isn't She Beautiful?
Wags and Kisses
A Perfect Christmas
Graduation: Just the Beginning!

Leaving Home

Survival of the Hippest

by Lynn Johnston and Andie Parton

Andrews McMeel
Publishing

Kansas City

For Better or For Worse is distributed by United Feature Syndicate.

www.FBorFW.com

05 06 07 RR2 10 9 8 7 6 5 4 3

Library of Congress Cataloging-in-Publication Data

Johnston, Lynn, 1947–

Leaving home : survival of the hippest / by Lynn Johnston and Andie Parton.

p. cm.

ISBN: 0-7407-3303-6

1. Young adults—United States—Life skills guides. I. Parton, Andie. II. Title.

HQ799.7.J64 2003

646.7'00842—dc21

2002045159

PART 1

Shelter: Be It Ever So Humble . . . There's No Place Like Home . . . 1

PART 2
Roommates: Crash Course in Compatibility . . . 27

PART 3
Feast and Famine: From "Fine Dining" to Food Banks—Striking a Balance . . . 53

PART 4
Budget Is Not a Four-Letter Word . . . 63

PART 5
Navigating Bureaucracy: Changing Your Address Without Going Postal . . . 73

PART 10
You, the Student . . . 131

PART 11
Parting Shots . . . 139

Leaving Home

Preface

Adrienne (Andie) Parton and I have been friends for thirty years. When we met, we were both single moms, surviving thanks to our children, our sense of humor, and welfare.

We have shared, leaned on, and learned from each other. Her family (Stephen, thirty-one, Christopher, twenty-nine, and Jennifer, twenty-three) grew up with music, laughter, and the ability to tell it like it is.

I thought her advice to our children as they left home, went to school, found work (and went to school again) was worth sharing. I asked if she would write a book—and typical of Andie—she came through.

—Lynn Johnston

Introduction

So you're heading out.

You've long dreamed of the day you'd leave home to start a new job or go to college, and this is it. Your future beckons and you're outta here.

This little guidebook will alert you to the potholes of life and will haul you out when you've seen the warning signs and fallen in anyway. After you've heard the folks' advice and ignored it, after you've built up your savings and blown it, after you left home but got lonesome the next day, then check out this last frontier of assistance, this "Manual of Mayday," this "Book of Help."

Herein lie the answers to the "Now What?" questions of life on your own: "I've blown the budget, now what?" "I've picked the roommate from hell, now what?" "Exams are over, we partied, I've been evicted, now what?"

Check this out; it could be the most valuable thing you're packing!

Part 1

Shelter: Be It Ever So Humble . . . There's No Place Like Home

Chapter 1

Finding It: Getting in on the Ground Floor of Apartment Hunting

Ah, my own place!" How many times have you tried those words on inside your head? Well, this time it's for real. Time to vacate the parental nest and find a place with *your* name on the door. Your new abode could be one of many possibilities: a room in someone's attic, a college campus residence, a house full of roommates, or an apartment on your own. Whether your finances are pointing you to a rooming house or a penthouse, you'll need to visit your future city well in advance to secure your new digs. Take a friend or a parent with you to lend their perspective. Their two cents' worth can prove invaluable (especially if it goes toward gas).

Before you take off, use the library or the Internet to check out the "For Rent" ads in the classified section of your new city's papers. Also, you'll find that many savvy educational institutions have made their housing info available on-line. In many cities, the housing notice board on the college/university campus is the prime advertising spot for area landlords. So whether you're a student or not, this

could be *the* place to start the search. You'll get an overview of availability, price, and the location of everything from single rooms to monster student houses.

If there's a glut of listings, advantage goes to the renter. This could mean lower rent or one month free. Note that "one month free" often means "Thirteenth month free." Try not to be loaded down with a twelve-month lease if you plan to dump your apartment before the summer months. Subletting can cause you grief if some yahoo takes over your place (since you are still responsible for it).

However, *renting a sublet* could be just the ticket for you. If you take over someone else's place at the end of a school year, you'll have a few months of cheaper rent with time to scope out the terrain.

The "Roommate Wanted" ads are another area to explore. Notice boards in every college and university are loaded with these, and you don't have to be a student to peruse them!

It's important to check out several places. (That means more than two!) You need to get a feel for what your housing allowance will score you. Check a potential place after dark: Who knows what comes out when the sun goes down? You need to be safe. If low rent buys you cockroaches and a back-alley entrance, you're going to need more cash. If rooms rent by the hour, pass.

You know what your needs are, but here are a few Q&As to help you choose what's right for you:

Q. Are you fresh out of high school and scared about being on your own? Worried about handling school, money, and hunger?

A. An on-campus residence will ease you into on-your-own living. If you're planning to study, this can be a good place. The fees cover utilities and food (with a meal plan), and the campus provides some modicum of security. And hopefully your "space" will give you some privacy.

Q. Are you pretty independent? Just want to look after yourself and get educated?

A. Off-campus apartments or rooms with kitchen and laundry facilities, with or without roommates, is what you're looking for.

Q. Do you have a deeply rooted need to live in a pack, where the music is loud, the couches are full, and sleep deprivation is a point of honor?

A. Off-campus student houses are for you. Later, when you're partied out and your grades have hit bottom, you can move to a cave and salvage your education.

The Lease

Read it—all of it! (This includes a campus residence agreement, not just an apartment lease.)

- Will you need to pay first and last months' rent? Does the rent include cable, parking, heat, or electricity? Fridge and stove?

- How much notice do you need to give before vacating early? (Premature evacuation?)
- What are the penalties for leaving early?
- Will management get huffy about your welding-sculpture hobby? Your hydroponics setup?
- What does the lease say about pets? Amazing that some people can't handle a lizard or two in their building . . .
- Is a damage deposit required?

Make sure that any preexisting problems are noted. Make a moving-in-day checklist so you don't get charged for old cigarette burns or missing doors. (If there's a fireplace in the house, you know where the doors went.) Conversely, tenants who are a little careless (read "destructive") don't usually insist on the first day walk-through. These guys always forfeit the damage deposits and are quite familiar with court orders. (You know who you are!)

In some places it's illegal for a landlord to require first and last months' rent as well as a damage deposit. Read up on tenant and landlord rights for your particular area (usually accessible on the Internet). Be aware but don't flaunt your knowledge to the landlord. No one likes a smart-ass; you'll know your stuff, but you'll also remain homeless.

File your copy of the lease somewhere and—this is tough—remember where you put it. This will come in handy later when you get your eviction notice. If there is no mention in the lease about keeping a colony of ferrets or working on your burned-out truck on the front lawn, then hey, what are they bugging you for?

Chapter 2

Furnishing It: Lining Your Nest

Mom's Basement Stuff: The Early Inheritance

If you're leaving on good terms with your family (if you rarely hear the words: "Never darken my doorway again"), then you can safely start furniture hunting in the parental abode. Tread lightly here; this is basically their stuff. You could say that their belongings are your inheritance, and you'll get these things eventually, but consider this: Your mom and dad are barely forty-five with several decades to go before they break up shop. Your kid sister will get the stock portfolio and you'll get the matching purple and green sofa-loveseat combo . . . so don't be grabby. It's probably safe to start with the room you're vacating.

Here are some "If's" to ponder while you're casing the joint:

- If a younger sibling is sharing your bedroom, you can't take all the furniture.

- If you are offered furniture and you don't like it, tough noogies; parents are under no obligation to shell out for more.
- If your parents let you sell some of their things, it's okay to buy new stuff with the proceeds, but make it house stuff.
- If you and your parents have spent their savings on schoolbooks and tuition, will it kill you to adopt milk crates as part of your decor?

Helping Your Neighbors: "Will Clear Your Attic of Furniture for Free!"

A lot of your neighbors have neat stuff stored under layers of cobwebs in their basements. Some of them would be happy to have their "treasures" moved to your new dwelling. A couple of days' labor could be all you need to line your nest. You may be asked to dispose of unusable items, so be prepared to visit the local dump, where you may find even more great stuff. Think positive here! Now spread the word. It helps if the neighborhood knows that you have older siblings who have already depleted the parental domain of available furnishings—sympathy works wonders. Post flyers at the supermarkets, stores, and laundromats nearby. Here's one to get you started:

WILL WORK FOR FURNITURE
Financially challenged student will clean your basement/attic/yard in return for your previously loved household furnishings, bed, desk, dresser, etc. References and truck available. Call Mike at 555-1234.

The Yard Sale = Your "Vintage Kitchenware Store"

A single Saturday morning of garage sale cruising can net you more than enough cutlery, bed linens, towels, curtains, black velvet paintings, lamps, dishes, couches, etc., for your apartment. Spring and autumn are the best times; look for neighborhood sales where the whole street gets into the game. Admit that you are just starting out on your own; feel free to ask how the slow cooker works; ask them to plug in the steam iron—no one minds. Go early and again late. Go early for more choices and late for lowered prices. No one is more willing to part with their leftovers than tired sellers at closing time. They'll throw mixing bowls, a toaster, and a complete (well, almost complete) set of dinnerware in a box for you to haul off their prop-

erty. Count on your stash to contain several diet books (now condemned by the FDA) and some eight-tracks of polka music.

Back-Alley Chic and Treasure Hunts

While you are desperately searching for the basic necessities, keep an eye out for those special decorator touches that will make your hovel truly a home:

- The railroad dining car sign for your bathroom door that says "Reserved for groups of 3 to 4"
- That "Yield" traffic sign you found in the gutter with your friends
- Specialty items like the almost-certainly-empty hornet's nest or that mummified bat you found

Special Garbage Days: Mark Your Calendar

You can really luck out on the spring and fall "Re-Userama Days." People drag out items not normally taken by the sanitation department (due to the size of the articles). These include anything from bed frames to couches to aquariums. People pickup is encouraged: Anyone can come along and help themselves. This is a very acceptable practice. In fact, you'll start bragging about your finds and set out every year like you're on some archaeological dig.

A call to the municipal office will tell you when the good townsfolk will haul your booty to their curb. Map out what neighborhood is scheduled on which day. (Exclude communities where the citizenry is chucking out items they gathered from the sidewalk last year.) The prime picking time is generally the night before "Collection Day."

Bring a couple of bodies and a borrowed wagon or, better still, a pickup truck. Whole apartments have been furnished and decorated this way. Perfectly good stereo systems have been rescued and have gone on to annoy many a neighbor. Leave mattresses and anything that looks inhabited. If appliances are not in good working order, a repair whiz isn't hard to find. If it can't be fixed, it may still be useful.

Moving Day: A View of Hell

Moving day is an adventure! It's the only way to look at it. You'll move several times in your life, and each move should be played for good laughs and great memories:

- You can never be too prepared for moving. Anal-retentive types fare best, as everything is precleaned, labeled, color-coded, and insured. Emulate them.

- Make yourself a care package ahead of time. Include toilet paper, a can opener, pen and paper, and foods needing no refrigeration or cooking (for when you forget to get the electricity hooked up). And a flashlight! Add a favorite childhood toy (just pretend your mom snuck it in).

- After the movers are gone, apologize to your new neighbors for the flattened flower beds, the rap music, the swearing, and the crud on the hall carpet.
- Blame everything on the movers; stress that they are strangers to you, just hired for the day.

At the end of the day, drop everything, step outside, and take a slow walk around. See the good stuff: the trees and the kids, the shops, and the dogs. The new neighborhood is now "yours."

Chapter 3

Decorating It: Friends, Paint, Tunes, and Beer

Moving to the wilds of the city can be scary, but a little fixing up can transform your new digs into a haven, your "port in the storm." Some cleaning and a few changes make the place "yours." If you're out of school and have a job, you may have more time (and desire) to revamp your little dump into cool-looking quarters, especially when the rent is right and you work close by. So if you're going to stay awhile and want to try your hand at decorating, here are a few pointers on finding help to get the job done:

- Start with getting the landlord to shell out for paint and stuff.
- If you have a sense of style and know how to apply that to your apartment, then all you need is a plan, some cash, and a work crew.
- If you lack imagination, then use someone else's. Look for ideas in decorating magazines; you'll find these at the library and the neighborhood garage sales, as well as in secondhand bookstores.
- Bring sketches or magazine pictures to a paint and wallpaper store. Most people are happy to dole out advice on their areas of expertise.
- Do you know someone whose taste you admire and who could help you devise a decorating plan?
- Be clear about what you can afford. You're probably skimming from the food budget, which means you're borrowing from the rent, so be careful.

Maybe you just need the place "spruced up." Perhaps the previous tenant's color scheme denoted a severe personality disorder. Or someone went berserk with Day-Glo spray paint, and you inherited the renovation job. In this case, let's first assume that you've negotiated a hefty rent discount from the landlord. You will then need a few good friends with muscle and perseverance, who hopefully owe you a favor. The offering of bribes is definitely in order.

Once you're solid on what needs to be done, then it's time to access your resources and recruit some bodies. When you clean up and change a place . . . it's "yours."

Your decorating resources:

- The library how-to-fix-and-decorate section (almost as useful as the adult literature section)
- Rental stores for everything from floor tarps to wallpaper steamers to expert advice
- Retired guys (Talent! Find one and make a new friend.)
- Loving relatives who will provide tools, elbow grease, and food
- Hardware stores that give classes and provide videos on decorating and repairs
- Schools of interior design with students who need you for their before-and-after projects (Take the risk!)
- Buddies from work or school for your decorating "party"

Stuff you'll need (borrow what you can):

- Spackle (or toothpaste, for really small repairs), a sander (with sandpaper), rags, tarps
- Paint, wallpaper, more than one brush, rollers, trays, chalk line reel, etc.

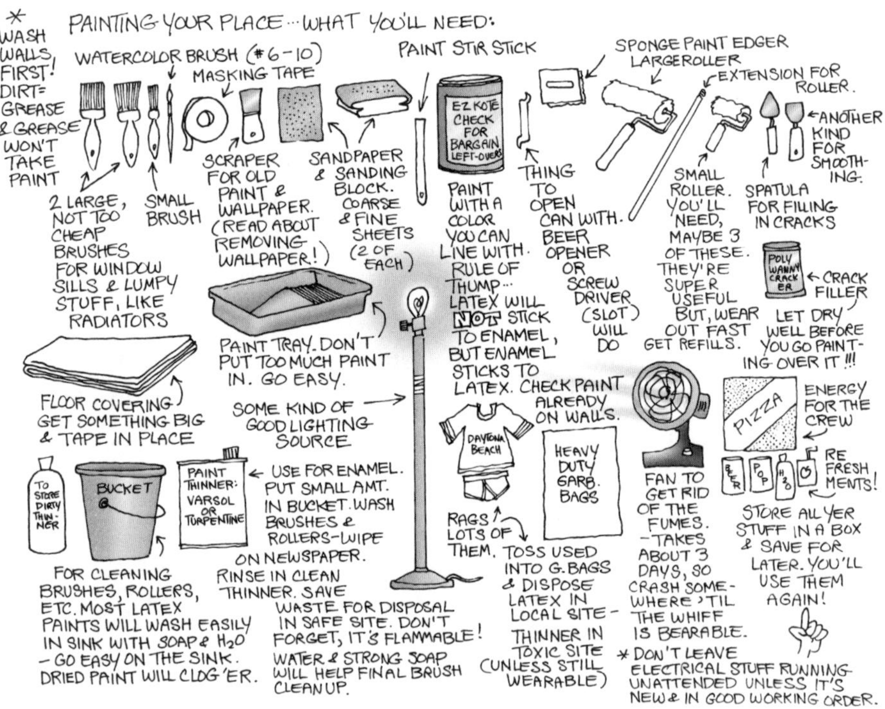

- Garbage bags, soap and water, broom, dustpan, paint cleaner (if brushes are to be reused with the same paint, wrap them in foil and stick them in the freezer till next use; it really works!)
- Top priority: Great stereo, beer, food, and workers of the opposite sex

The Paint Party:

- Prepare the area: Empty it; clean it.
- Be ready to start when the people arrive. Have all equipment on hand—no searching for a ladder at the last minute.

- Pick a foreman. (You may not be the best choice to order your volunteer friends around.)
- Keep the beer cold and the pizza hot.
- Let your crew choose the music.
- To avert disaster, check work often; make the foreman address mistakes, not you.
- You may be stuck with the cleanup job. Live with it.
- Admire everyone's handiwork. Thank your friends profusely.
- Repeat your offers of reciprocation (and keep your promises); say good-bye.
- Air the place out.
- Now uncrate your things: your books, your pictures, your comic book collection, or your Barbie dolls. Spread your stuff around. Doesn't it feel like home! Doesn't it feel like yours?

Chapter 4

Keeping It: The Eviction Notice—a Rite of Passage

Question: If the riot police make an appearance at your little soiree, can the eviction notice be far behind?

So the neighbors were not amused when the SWAT team showed up at your party last night. Or did the wet T-shirt contest on the front lawn tick them off? Maybe not paying your rent (yet again) was the final straw. Whatever. The landlord has called your last strike and you're out!

What are you going to do with your very own eviction notice? Well, you could A) fight it, B) ignore it, or C) obey it.

Fighting It

There is only one way: apologies and reparation. You can't pretend the transgressions didn't happen; there were many witnesses to the couch-chucking-off-the-balcony incident. But following the couch with your old fridge, well, that sealed your fate. Yes, getting them down to the curb three floors below was too complicated, but what were you thinking? Maybe a written apol-

ogy and paying for repairs to everyone's balconies could get your walking papers rescinded. Good luck!

Ignoring It

Maybe the landlady was bluffing. Maybe if you clean everything up and lie low for a while this will go away. Unlikely, but worth a try. It will be interesting to see what comes first: an irate landlady, escorted by a few hulks with a Dumpster, or a set of new tenants at your door, complete with furniture and a signed lease. Your call.

Obeying It

Could be there's no way out but out. Either the offense was beyond repair or you've been issued so many warnings that it's useless to fight the inevitable. Sober up, straighten out, and move on.

The Landlord from Hell

Sometimes a landlord is impossible to deal with, no matter how rule-abiding the tenants. These landlords/superintendents spy on you, enter your place without permission, show it to others with no warning, and even threaten you. Forget a bag of garbage in the hall just once and you'll find the dreaded warning letter in your mailbox. Have your brother visit overnight from out of town and it's considered a major infraction. These landlords can be loud and rude and downright scary. Sometimes you can't win. This is one of the few instances when a lease-breaking blowout could be in order.

Chapter 5

Leaving It: Seven Ways to Leave Your Landlord

You've made a commitment and signed a lease, but your best buddy just landed an incredible apartment for both of you. It's big and warm and close to everything, and your pal needs your answer now! Your place is cramped, ugly, and costs more, so there's no question: It's time to go. But, how do you go? How do you avoid those lease-breaking penalties? Just slip out the back, Jack . . .

1. Post a PYTHON MISSING flyer in the front lobby; an invitation to find accommodations elsewhere will soon follow.
2. Lie: Your clan fell on hard times and you must go tend to the farm before birthing season. (Note this is not the honorable thing to do.)
3. Make a predawn escape (not a citizen-of-the-year deed either); this should be reserved for the landlord from hell.
4. Sublet; install cousin Bradley till the lease runs out.
5. Try the truth and throw yourself on the mercy of the landlord. Maybe he wants your apartment for his niece and will let you off with a minimal penalty.
6. Not all landlords are subhumans, but if yours is *and* you've lucked onto a great new place, the lease-breaking bash could be the thing.
7. *Or* (the shocker): Scratch up some bucks, pay the penalty, and set yourself free!

Chapter 6

Cleaning It: Keeping the Health Department at Bay

You're walking home after an evening of pizza and movies at your friend's place and you can't shake off the feeling that something was weird about his apartment. Then you walk into your place and, with the swiftness for which you are famous, it hits you—his was clean!

Face it: In your "on my own" fantasies, the cleanup clause got buried in the small print. Just like noise bylaws and late-payment penalties.

Folks have different notions of clean. Some people actually make regular efforts. They wash off the omelet before it becomes a permanent part of the frying pan and their shower stalls get hosed down before sandblasting is required. If this is you, you are greatly admired. Please skip to the next chapter.

The "misunderstood" occupy an apartment till the garbage reaches the windows, then they simply move out. They have difficulty with references from landlords. Try not to date them!

Then there's the binge cleaner, the regular "I just cleaned up a month ago, I can't believe it's dirty again" guy/girl: This chapter is for you.

There may be hints that the joint needs cleaning: The telephone number written in the dust by the phone is three boyfriends old. Flies are wintering in your kitchen and you're starting to give them names. And furthermore, your assignments are on time and you handed in your last essay before the due date. Meaning, of course, that your apartment is a sty. This will never do. When the corner gas station bathroom is more appealing than yours, it's time to bond with a scrubbing brush.

Finding "The Zone" in the world of clean:

- You do well if the cleanup job is a competition, like "Beat the Clock"? Great. Set a timer, pick a room, and go! If the room is cleaned before your, say, thirty minutes are up, you get a prize! A beer maybe, or, okay, Dairy Queen.

- Are deadlines your great motivators? Then set yourself one: two hours before the hockey game begins, fire up the vacuum, prime that spray cleaner, and get going!
- Cleaning as exercise! Stretch, climb, run—whatever cranks you. But have a feather duster in your hand while you sweat it out!
- Cleaning as therapy. Never waste a good snit! Been dumped? Scrub till the real bathroom floor emerges. Didn't get the job? Give that greased-up stove a new life.
- Multitasking. Time your duty phone calls with any gross cleanup job. You could shine up a whole kitchen *and* lend an ear to Aunt Margie's latest surgical ordeal. Invest in a long phone cord.

- The Last Resort: Invite people over! Difficult people: your boss, your teacher, your boyfriend's mother. Guaranteed to "Zone" you into a garbage collecting frenzy!

Your basic cleaning equipment:

- Rags: Cut-up T-shirts or old underwear is great. (Wash them first.)
- Broom, dustpan, and whisk broom: These can even be used on carpets if you are vacuum-deprived.
- Feather duster: Anything on a stick that collects dust and doesn't just blow it around.
- Sponges with scrubber on one side: For scrubbing sinks and tubs, these babies really get the job done.
- Four containers:

  One for soapy water to scrub floors.

  One for fresh water to rinse.

  One for garbage: Line with grocery bag, carry from room to room, and . . . pick up the garbage. (Put a wad of empty bags in bottom of the pail so that a new bag will happen when the first bag is full.)

  One for stuff: To avoid seventeen trips with items destined for other rooms.
- Spray bottle: Make your own glass cleaner with water and vinegar; use with paper towels or newspapers.
- Rubber gloves: Decrease the gross factor and save the manicure.
- Scrub brush, sponge mop, and old toothbrushes if you care about those "hard to reach places."
- And for extreme cases, a power-washer and a biohazard suit!

Cleaners (It's worth reading these directions. Honest!):

- All-purpose liquid cleaner: First purchase in a spray bottle, then buy the cheap refill containers.
- Cream cleanser: This doesn't just pour down the drain like liquid; it's great with a sponge/scrubber in the bathroom and kitchen.

THE CLEANING ESSENSHULS

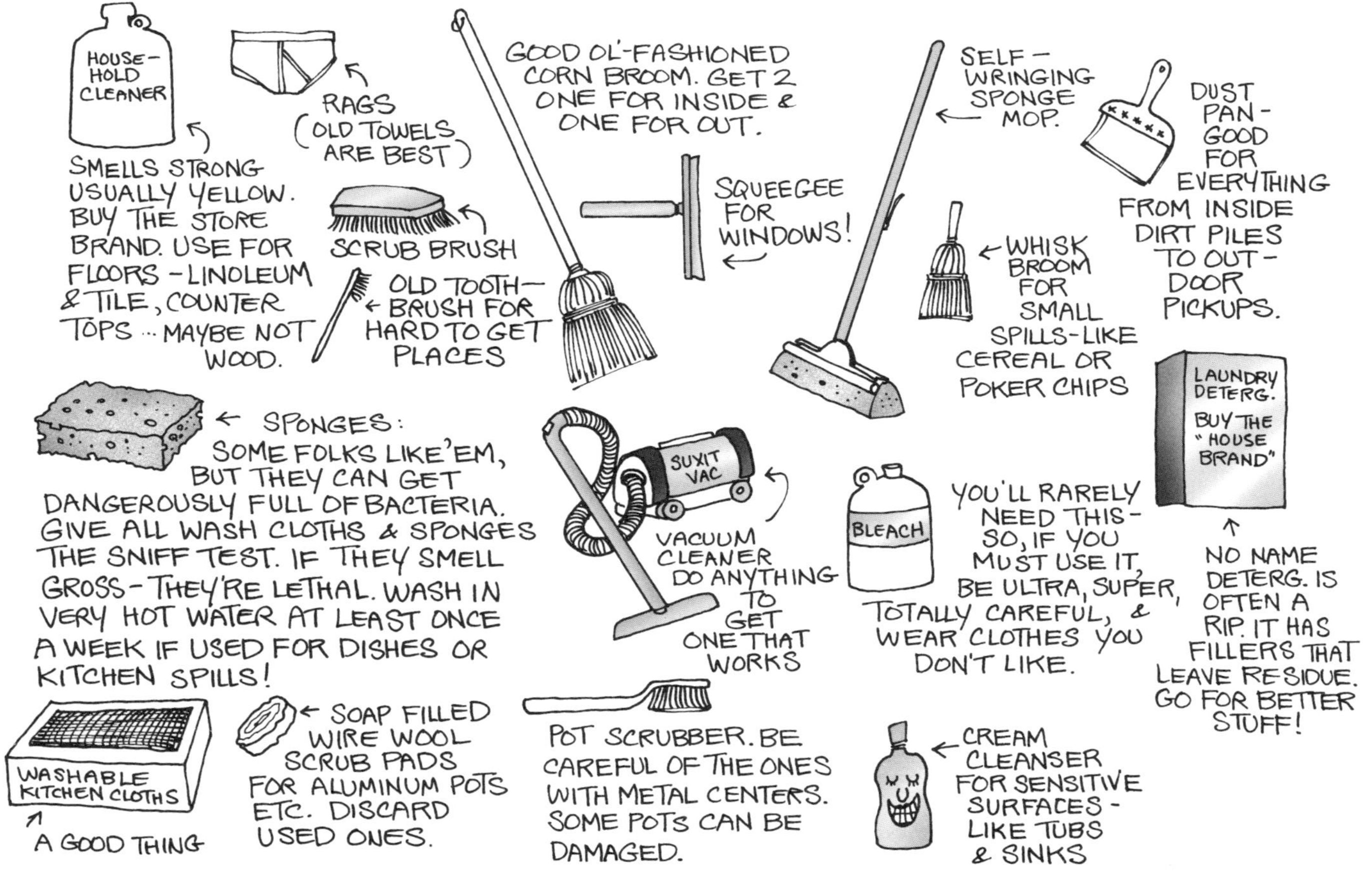

HOUSE-HOLD CLEANER

SMELLS STRONG USUALLY YELLOW. BUY THE STORE BRAND. USE FOR FLOORS – LINOLEUM & TILE, COUNTER TOPS ... MAYBE NOT WOOD.

RAGS (OLD TOWELS ARE BEST)

SCRUB BRUSH

OLD TOOTH-BRUSH FOR HARD TO GET PLACES

GOOD OL'-FASHIONED CORN BROOM. GET 2 ONE FOR INSIDE & ONE FOR OUT.

SQUEEGEE FOR WINDOWS!

SELF-WRINGING SPONGE MOP.

WHISK BROOM FOR SMALL SPILLS-LIKE CEREAL OR POKER CHIPS

DUST PAN-GOOD FOR EVERYTHING FROM INSIDE DIRT PILES TO OUT-DOOR PICKUPS.

SPONGES: SOME FOLKS LIKE 'EM, BUT THEY CAN GET DANGEROUSLY FULL OF BACTERIA. GIVE ALL WASH CLOTHS & SPONGES THE SNIFF TEST. IF THEY SMELL GROSS – THEY'RE LETHAL. WASH IN VERY HOT WATER AT LEAST ONCE A WEEK IF USED FOR DISHES OR KITCHEN SPILLS!

SUXIT VAC

VACUUM CLEANER DO ANYTHING TO GET ONE THAT WORKS

BLEACH

YOU'LL RARELY NEED THIS – SO, IF YOU MUST USE IT, BE ULTRA, SUPER, TOTALLY CAREFUL, & WEAR CLOTHES YOU DON'T LIKE.

LAUNDRY DETERG. BUY THE "HOUSE BRAND"

NO NAME DETERG. IS OFTEN A RIP. IT HAS FILLERS THAT LEAVE RESIDUE. GO FOR BETTER STUFF!

WASHABLE KITCHEN CLOTHS

A GOOD THING

SOAP FILLED WIRE WOOL SCRUB PADS FOR ALUMINUM POTS ETC. DISCARD USED ONES.

POT SCRUBBER. BE CAREFUL OF THE ONES WITH METAL CENTERS. SOME POTS CAN BE DAMAGED.

CREAM CLEANSER FOR SENSITIVE SURFACES – LIKE TUBS & SINKS

- Bleach: Let it sit in the toilet and tub (diluted, approximately one cup to a tub of water, *above* the dirt line) while you do other things—twenty minutes or so. Throw in the floor mop; it cleans up "real well."
- Any gadgetry your budget can handle. (Avoid battery-powered mini-vacs. They suck—but not enough!)

How to clean:

1. Pick a room. Pick the cleanest one and get it done; this will give you a sense of accomplishment. Rotate your starting point, or you'll burn out at the same room each time and eventually it'll have to be carted off to the dump.
2. Scan the room. View it through a stranger's eyes. You may be too close to your mess; maybe that CONDEMNED BY THE HEALTH DEPARTMENT sign is already in your mail. Which pile would that be? A stranger would sense that your tub wasn't dirt-colored when it left the factory. And that the corner love seat is actually a mummified stack of take-out boxes. (A stranger might also notice that your friend Mel is a freeloader and should also be dragged to the curb.) Sometimes one doesn't notice one's own chaos.
3. Move the dirt downward.
   - Bring your cleaning gear, garbage pail, and "stuff" container into the room.
   - Put loose garbage into pail (leave glued-on garbage for now) and set the pail outside the room.
   - All items not residing in this room go into the "stuff" container. Fine, move the fridge back into the kitchen, if that's where it belongs. Set the container outside the room—contents to be put away later.
   - Dust from the top down. Special dusters trap dust instead of swirling it around, and also are easy on the TV screen. Dust furniture, side tables, lamps, dressers, desks, shelves, etc. Shake the duster into a closed trash bag, not off the balcony

into the neighbors' windows; yes, you're supposed to shake out the dirty duster.

- Wash surfaces with a damp cloth and all-purpose spray cleaner: railings, baseboards (isn't this going a little far?), doorways, cupboards. Rinse. For all those glued-on remains, as well as kitchen and bath countertops, sinks, showers, and tub (after the bleaching), use the cream cleanser and the sponge/scrubber combo. Rinse. Same with the toilet. Get a brush for toilet bowl cleaning, and don't use the toilet rags in the kitchen, okay?
- Almost done. Sweep the floor and mop/rinse it. If you don't have a vacuum cleaner for the carpet, sweep it hard or borrow the neighbor's vacuum. You can find a cheap carpet sweeper at the local flea market; they really work.
- Ta da! Take a break, then on to the next room.
- Finally, take out the garbage (check garbage arrangements; no early curb placement for dogs and raccoons to spread around), replace all stuff to its home, and put cleaning things away. Toss the rags in the laundry or spread them out to dry.

Still, life happens; if your priorities include playing and making a living and getting a degree, and whatever it takes to achieve world peace, well, then, the following is for you:

Best Mess Line

Consider the words of the harassed housewife whose mother-in-law arrived without warning. In a stroke of brilliance, the daughter-in-law surveyed her very messy home and announced:

"We've just been vandalized and the police said not to touch a thing!"

Feel free to adopt this line as your own.

Part 2

Roommates: Crash Course in Compatibility

Chapter 7

Finding Them: From Stalking the Laundromats to Eavesdropping on the Bus

Newspaper Ad:

Roommate Wanted

"Newly renovated, furnished room, would suit mature female; must love animals, Christian home, no lease."

Could mean . . .

"I've slapped a coat of paint on the walls of my back room and covered the mystery stains with an area rug. I dragged the old cot and folding chair up from the basement and reclaimed an orange desk from the firewood. You must be at least thirty-five years old. I am a single middle-aged lady with twelve cats. This is a religious home. No smoking, drinking, swearing, sex, or attitude will be tolerated. You may be asked to leave at any time. No males need apply."

So you thought finding compatible roommates was going to be easy! Not likely! If you're covering the rent solo in a big house or if you're still at the folks' where the welcome mat is getting thin, *tempus fugit*, baby, time is flying. Here's the heads-up for your search.

Where Do You Start?

Well first, what's your deal?

1. Are you a roommate in need of a place?
2. Or do you have a place in need of a roommate?

Whatever; help is at hand.

Try the word-of-mouth search and if that gets you nowhere, then give the want ads a try. Mostly, here's how it works:

- You need the room? You *check* the ads.
- You have the room? You *place* the ad.

Conduct your search carefully. It's a pain: if there's a job to go to or teachers to harass, you have little time for hunting down the perfect roommate. But your success away from home may well depend on how sweet your roommate situation is, so make the time.

Where to Place/Find Ads

University/College Housing Boards (Free!)

Student housing offices are a good place to start. Landlords provide their off-campus info to the college, and the housing office posts it on their boards and Web sites. This includes requests for roommates. Staff will help with printouts, maps, and advice. See if your tuition gets you a bus pass along with your degree. Living farther away is cheaper, but travel costs can eat the difference.

Some school housing services have telephones and computers for you to use in your search. You could show up with your worldly goods, check the board, access the Web site, print your faves, park yourself at a phone, and be in your new place before the first afternoon soap.

If you're not a student and want to use the school's housing information, note that some landlords require their tenants to be students, even demanding written proof. (Maybe they need the break in the summer.) What's wrong with a young person with a paying job?

As if you weren't a wholesome beer-swigging party animal like any student. Ask. Some schools won't allow landlords to restrict nonstudents. Good.

Newspaper Ads (Not Free)

Here's the thing about newspaper editors: By adhering to the human rights laws regarding race and creed, they are protecting people, including you, from discrimination. So you can't advertise for a roommate of a particular race or religion, age or marital status, with or without offspring, etc. (but it's okay to request your smoking preference). On the gender issue, there are a few ways you can justify advertising for same-sex roommates, for example, if the bathroom facilities need to be shared. Presumably, no one will come checking!

You can't write that you *don't* want a particular race or religion.

"No over-thirty Wicca-practicing Caucasian males with kids need apply." However you do have the right to a degree of comfort within your living quarters. What you *can* say is what you are: "3 Korean female engineering students have 4-bedroom house to share with same." (The word "same" might be questioned.) Certainly the Korean students and the old white guy with the witchcraft rituals and his three teens might be happier apart. But preventing their cohabitation is a job for the screening call or interview, not for the newspaper.

So, the ad in the paper provides the generalities. The specifics need to come out in a telephone call or a face-to-face interview (see chapter 8).

More Places to Read or Place Ads

"Roommate Wanted" ads are common on notice boards in laundromats, supermarkets, churches, community centers, and your workplace. Check the lobbies of apartment buildings you'd like to live in. For your own ad, get permission and get your flyer posted.

Roommate Referral Services

It's worth checking the Internet and the good ol' yellow pages for referral services in your area. For a fee, they will match "rentors" with "rentees." With these services, you can be more specific about your needs than in the newspapers. Reasonable requests like compatible sleeping habits, food quirks, cleaning compulsions, and addictions to jazz will be fired into the "match-o-matic." Be sure to come clean about hobbies like mouse breeding, saxophone playing, or anything involving leather.

Building an Ad: Gotta Make Them Want You!

Some truths to enhance:

- Any electronics you own that involve viewing, listening, and cyber-travel: "Have 2-bedroom basement rat hole; will share satellite dish (all-sports channels, all-music video channels), video games, and high-speed Internet." (Rented ten minutes after the newspaper is on the stand!)
- Beer fridge on veranda.

Then you've got your usual:

- Proximity to school or work: "5 min. to IBM building." (Your last roommate, the marathon runner, made it in just four minutes, forty-three seconds.)
- Spacious. (Although maybe not so much after you put the furniture in.)

Some truths to avoid:

- The bingo hall downstairs is open twenty-four hours a day.
- The only real antiques in your building are the furnace and the landlady.
- You live downwind from the rendering (road-kill recycling) plant.
- Popular yard ornament in your neighborhood? Crime scene tape!

Putting it together:
State what you've got and what you'll charge for it:

- *The accommodations (basic layout):* 5-bedroom student house; 3-bedroom high-rise apt.; duplex; etc.
- *The amenities (nice to have):* private entrance, laundry, parking, close to . . . , own bathroom, etc.
- *The goodies (you wish!):* Jacuzzi, hot tub, fireplace, pool table, stereo, cable, big-screen TV, etc.
- *The rent:* Investigate and compare. All things being equal, split what you're paying among the group. *But* if you are to be the rent collector and the bill payer and the "One Who Deals with the Landlord When the Crap Hits the Fan," then your rent share should be at least 10 percent to 20 percent less than the others. (Unless your new mate will be living in the closet under the stairs. Play fair.)
- *The utilities:* If it winds you up to nag your forgetful housemates every month for the gas bill money, knock yourself out. Or, call the electricity, heat, and water people and ask them for user costs for the last few years. Find a monthly average and divide by your roomies; add this to each one's rent and voilà: "Utilities Included."

This is what you've got so far:
"Roommate Wanted: Student house, 5 bedrooms (2 available), laundry, parking, 2 min. walk to Glendale subway, Internet hook-up, $400 incl. utilities."

The only thing left is getting who you want.

How do your word your ad? Remember that you're looking for a housemate, not a life partner. Just give some thought to what you're into, what you value, what you need. Put that in your ad and someone simpatico should come knocking.

"Serious chemistry student . . ."
"Serious sports fan, dish, big-screen TV . . ."
"Failing 2nd-year physics, need tutor; rent negotiable . . ."

"'Happening' student house needs bossy den mother/person to keep landlord from giving last notice . . ."

"Botanist/naturalist—live snakes welcome . . ."

"I work days, like quiet; shift worker welcome…"

"Dance music, party central . . ."

"Theater arts students, high drama . . ."

Check out the ads below. They describe the same place with different needs and different toys: "weekly blowout" versus "serious student"; satellite dish versus bedroom Internet. No ambiguity here. Both "Chris" and "Terry" will get someone they can live with.

Roommate Wanted

A) 3-bedroom apartment, 5 min. walk to college, crawling distance to day/night clinic, laundry, cable, GameCube, weekly party, satellite dish. Pet OK. $300 incl. utilities. Call Chris at 444-555-1234.

B) 3-bedroom apartment, 5 min. walk to college, high-speed Internet (with hookup in your room), laundry; 3rd-year serious science student. Pet OK. $300 incl. utilities. Call Terry at 444-555-1234.

It's time to make contact with the strangers who will share your air. You'll swap stories and dance politely around each other. This is more than just divvying up the rent; you could be acquiring a fan of your obscure mandolin tapes, the rock-climbing partner you've been seeking, or an actual friend. And many roommates who rejoice in each other's positives (like great street parties with multiple cop showings), as well as negatives (for example, pregnancy tests), remain in each other's lives long after the last eviction.

Chapter 8

Screening Them: Weeding Out the Psycho Roommate Is Harder Than You Think

Real-life roommate screening goes like this: A body shows up with rent money and there's your guy! No wonder so many horror movies seem to describe ex-housemates. There's gotta be a way to keep the roommate-from-hell far from your space.

Check your prospectives out on the phone first; this saves everyone's time. If the distance is too far, the rent too high or the feel is wrong, you'll sense it; you'll know. If it's a possible, then it's face-to-face contact time: "Come over and see the place," which means "Come over and let's check each other out" (called the "sniff and wag").

You'll ask open-ended questions, which require more than a "yes" or "no," and you'll do the listening; what you hear might help you separate the nut-bars from the dialed-in. Asking about school and work, music and sports can bring out priorities of quiet and studying versus parties and noise. You want a few signs that "this bud's for you!"

Roommates who don't make the cut:

Shows up with parole officer.
Wants the first month free.
Their odor lingers long after the meeting is over.
Offers you a joint.
Maimed their last roommate.
She, Beethoven. You, rap.
Your dog, who loves everyone, snarls through the whole visit.
Has his mother interview you.
First words: "That wallpaper really sucks!"
You get that "bad feeling."

Roommates who make the A-list:

Shows up with a rent check.
Has a working vehicle.
Still has good standing with the video store (unlike the rest of you).
Offers you a joint.

Speaks Spanish! (Or Russian, or French, or . . . Will it rub off on you?) New culture, new insights, new food!
Comes with monthly care package and will share.
Works out of town (for those who feel that a good roommate is an absent roommate).
Owns a stereo.
Great clothing style; looks just your size.
You get that "good feeling."

You, the new roommate:
If you want the gig, (and you've checked out other places), offer a deposit.
If you don't want to live there, say that you have other places to see, thank you, and good-bye.

You, the one with the apartment:
If you want this roommate, say so (although you really should sleep on it).
If you don't, say that more people are scheduled for later; you'll make a decision in a few days.

Sometimes it seems that picking a roommate is a crapshoot.

Allison sounded neat over the phone, so Jody arranged to meet her. She arrived in all her glory: lip ring, tongue stud, multiple hair colors and accompanied by her mom, the local tattoo artist. Scared the heck out of Jody, for a minute. Allison also had a killer smile, a great attitude, and a steady job. Jody got a good feeling about her moving in, handed her a key to the apartment, and they've been buddies ever since!

Now check this out:

Mike was working on his engineering degree and needed a quiet place. That was just fine with Chris; he needed to keep his grades up and welcomed a roommate with the same goals.

Unfortunately, Mike argued about everything from day one. He also didn't appear to know how to work the shower. The air stank; the relationship was strained. Mike's tenure was short and not sweet.

People are like a box of chocolates . . .
Stay careful. Stay open.

Chapter 9

Dumping Them: So You Skipped the Screening Chapter . . .

Well it's just not working out. That's what happens when one roommate irons the face cloths while the other washes dishes "as needed"; one is a heavy-metal night owl while the other greets the dawn with surround-sound military music; one prepays the cable bill, the other coughs up rent money three weeks into next month . . . doomed from the start!

Before giving your roommate the heave-ho, it might be useful to do a little soul searching. Could the real reason that your relationship's in the toilet be:

- You're an even bigger slob than she is? (How embarrassing!)
- You forgot to lay down some ground rules and now it's too late?
- Your new sweetie thinks your roomie is hot?
- You've had ten roommates and hated them all?
- *You're* having yet another bad day?

If you answer yes to any of these questions, then the problem could possibly be about you, and not much about your roommate; in this case, you have three options:

1. Work on your attitude and keep the roommate.
2. Start fresh with a new attitude and a new roommate.
3. Live alone.

If you and your roommate have irreconcilable differences then the only question is: Who goes?

Scenario #1: Roomie Stays, You Go

Things to consider if you're going to be the one to leave:

- Did you sign a lease? Can you find the lease?
- What does the fine print say about notice times and penalties for leaving before your due date? You could be blessed with a landlord with long waiting lists who doesn't get excited about these small details.
- Maybe you can replace yourself. Don't you have some old acquaintance/enemy who would make a perfect match for your soon-to-be-ex-roommate?
- Consider also that your cohabitant may be itching to see you pack and will make concessions for your early departure.
- Once you've become aware of your lease obligations, communicate somehow with your roommate. Calmly state your plan. Expect a few stressful days or even weeks before you can exit.

Scenario #2: Roomie Goes, You Stay

If you're chained to your lease and you have to stay, or this is your dream place and you *want* to stay, things can get tense. You're going to have to ask your roommate to leave. Isn't confrontation fun? Choose your words carefully. Will hurt feelings translate into the "Australian Surprise" on your next month's phone bill? Or the "Delayed Hard

Drive Super Fry Virus"? Keep your cool and watch your manners.

Maybe you can lie about your cousin Wanda needing to move in with her three kids. Or you could be truthful and discuss your incompatibility and how both of you deserve better. This could be a very difficult conversation, one that most adults are unable to pull off. You should rehearse your talk and eliminate any put-downs and accusations. State your position; you can't handle the noise, fighting, late rent, mess, scary friends, drinking, doping . . . whatever it is that's making you crazy. After you've said your piece, take a deep breath and then: "You'll have to move out." If words get confrontational, a good tactic is to restate your position: You can't handle the noise, etc. Remember, whatever you say, be calm, firm, and respectful, 'cause more important even than retrieving the apartment key or getting cash for the electric bill is *getting your CDs back!*

Finally, if there is a blow-up and things get ugly, get some level-headed buddy over to calm things down. Resist the impulse to hold belongings for ransom till whatever is yours gets forked over.

You may need to pack up your now ex-roommate's belongings, pile them outside the door, and have the locks changed. Or if you're the one exiting, you may find yourself homeless, carrying garbage bags and looking for a friend with a sympathetic ear and a free couch. Expect some rough days ahead. There are big lessons to be learned here, and once is enough!

Chapter 10

Enjoying Them: First, *Be* a Good Roommate . . .

You've left the mother ship and taken up residence with other escapees. Your duty now is to create for yourself "A Most Excellent Roommate Experience." Just think—you're building a collection of memories to impress your future grandkids and upset their nervous parents.

The truth is that life with roommates can be dicey. To prep yourself heading into it, check out these four "Tools for Life": *communication, manners, rules, and fun*. See if they don't make this time amazing. And here's a bonus: Many people count among their lifelong friends the strangers they shared apartments with in their youth.

Communication

Can you spot Jenny and Melissa's little communication snafu here?

> *Jenny rents out a bedroom to Melissa, a girl from work who answered her "Roommate Wanted" ad. Jenny knows, in her mind, that the paltry, pathetic amount she got for the rent entitles Melissa merely to a bedroom and the use of the kitchen/bathroom/laundry facilities for a few select hours a day. She can occasionally watch TV, but only if she's a soap fan.*
>
> *Melissa answered Jenny's "Roommate Wanted" ad, and knows, in her mind, that the major cash she dished out to Jenny for her rent entitles her to pretty-well the run of the house and her choice of TV programs, music, and video games.*

Now sit back and watch the tension rise! Like the prison warden said to his rebellious prisoner (Paul Newman) in that old movie *Cool Hand Luke* (check it out!): "What we have here is failure to commun'cate."

Discussion can prevent demolition.

Manners

Has anyone ever hinted that you were ill-mannered? You scoff at the thought. You know how to hold a teacup properly, if you must; you can handle yourself in any posh eaterie; what's that got to do with your roomies? Okay, you're the prince of etiquette, but it's the Please's and Thank-you's, the Pardon me's, and the No, you go first's that will make life pleasant back at the ranch.

Good manners are simply politeness with heart.

It's a cruel world out there. Don't bring it home. Every day someone flashes their dark side at you: Salesclerks get rude and road ragers cut you off. That's bad manners. You've heard of soccer rage? Bad manners on steroids. Here's a big one: Pearl Harbor! In fact, it is said that whole wars would have been averted if only for a display of good manners!

"Good manners are the glue of society," said the great philosopher Kramer from TV's *Seinfeld*. And that's just what you former strangers need: something to stick you together.

It's good manners to familiarize yourself with the customs of roommates who grew up in cultures different than your own. (Imagine the major efforts for someone adapting to *your* culture!) This is what tolerance and openness are: just your basic good manners. Treating people with kindness will get you up and over a lot of high fences!

You have roommates now; go practice on them.

Rules

No, you don't want to cramp your style with rules, but read on. You make rules to prevent chaos and you make rules for the benefit of all. Understand that there are lots of problems that you *won't* have because you've set up a few rules. Now here's the good part: It's *you* making the rules—not just you alone, but you're in!

Rules for making rules:

- Keep the list short.
- Make the rules self-explanatory. ("Keep the noise down in the daytime Mondays and Tuesdays; Joe works nights.")
- Set up rules together: People are more inclined to follow rules when they've had a hand in making them. ("Oh yeah, I made that silly cleanup rule, didn't I?")
- Get formal. Write them up. Stick them on the fridge door, near the chore list. Fridge door rules eliminate the "It's not my turn," "I forgot when the cable is due," "I did it last week." So, any questions, check the fridge!

- Discuss rules with new roommates before they sign up (as part of the screening). Be open to changing or deleting. Sometimes a good rule can be made better.
- Set up a regular time for beefs and general whining. You got problems? Show up with solutions. Try new things. (In one apartment, after two months of unsuccessful attempts at following the cleaning rules, the consensus was: "We are pigs; we are happy in our mess." What worked? Before a date or a parent arrived, major cleanup by all!)

Call them HOUSE RULES, then nobody has to be the heavy.

What kind of rules?

- Work rules: who does what, and when.
- Money rules: who pays for what, how much, and when.
- Social rules: everything else—sex, drugs, and rock 'n' roll.

Up for discussion:

- Splitting the food bill; fine if you all have the same tastes, appetite, and budget.
- Buying your own; okay, but now the fridge is filled with sour milk and four open bottles of ketchup. And thirty-two rolls of toilet paper are piled outside the bathroom.
- So how about building a list of the common stuff—the relish, mayo, floor cleaner, garbage bags, and lightbulbs, for starters; and the group addictions—Sugar Krudds, high-octane pop, corn chips, and beer. Whoever has the kitchen gig then monitors the "gotta have" list.
- On rent day, everyone puts a set amount of money into the kitty, or potty, or whatever warped idea comes to mind to stash cash in, for the "stuff" list (an honor system).
- Consider letting people do what they like: Tina likes to clean but hates cooking. Mike likes to cook. Tina is the happy scrubber and eats anything Mike cooks. Jason, the numbers man, handles the

bills and is Tina and Mike's willing backup guy. A grateful bunch with no chore list.

- How long can boyfriends/girlfriends stay? You'll rule together on this touchy subject—rules that you'll promptly ignore the minute you finally land a true love of your own. But love/lust can be fleeting. A change of heart and you want your space back. Now here's where the rules look after you: "It's the rules, see; no extra guests allowed, see"; and bingo, you're liberated. (Lying to your now ex-friend is another matter; right now we're dealing with house rules.)

Tried and truisms:

- Frequent guests become paying guests.
- Better to look dorky with rules up front than to try setting up a beer rule *after* your roommates drink all of yours. Don't assume that roommates will be considerate.
- When too many telephone charges have no owners, it's time to cancel long-distance services and have everyone buy their own prepaid call cards.
- Friends who decide to become roommates sometimes need rules more than strangers do; she, whose life philosophies match your own, makes you crazy with her hour-long showers and smelly leftovers. What are you going to do now?
- Confronting a delinquent roommate (loud, messy, boozy, late with rent, etc.) is scary and stressful. Be straight up! Say it: "You're a slob, man. We're fed up. Clean up your act! Okay, now we're ordering pizza, what do you want on it?" There! Or you could all live for months with tension and resentment. Cowards!
- A chronic rule breaker is someone who doesn't want to live with you anymore. See the light.

Sample Rules

HOUSE RULES

(Let's say for Angela, David, and Joseph)

- Clean up after yourself; your mother doesn't live here.
- For the areas we all mess up, there's some anal-type cleaning chart on the fridge. Take turns. One week at a time. Just do it.
- Angela gets the rent money, 1st of the month, checks made out to her. She gets nasty, don't be late.
- David ("Don't call me Dave!") handles the utility bills; checks due on the 20th.
- Joseph "The Gentleman" is the telephone guy; bill due on the 25th. He will be courteous while damaging your dialing finger; pay up.
- Don't let your guests behave like jerks.
- Respect your roomies' privacy and space. Not sure? Just ask.
- Max is too fat and is now cut off ribs and wings; Joe will feed him, it's *his* cat.

Sample Chore Chart

Who Does What When?							
WHEN	October 1–7	October 8–14	October 15–21	October 22–28	October 29–November 4	November 5–11	November 12–18
WHO	WHAT	WHAT	WHAT	WHAT	WHAT	WHAT	WHAT
JOSEPH	Kitchen	Bathroom	Living Room/ Hall	Kitchen	Bathroom	Living Room/ Hall	Kitchen
DAVID	Bathroom	Living Room/ Hall	Kitchen	Bathroom	Living Room/ Hall	Kitchen	Bathroom
ANGELA	Living Room/ Hall	Kitchen	Bathroom	Living Room/ Hall	Kitchen	Bathroom	Living Room/ Hall

Rules you never thought you'd have to make:

- Rent is not a voluntary contribution.
- Houseplants are not to be smoked.
- The landlord must be invited to *all* parties.
- The goat is cute but he'll have to go.
- Roommate nudity is *not* required.
- Whoever breeds the bugs owns the exterminator bill.
- No shopping in your roommates' closets.
- By Tuesday, the Friday night kegger should be winding down.
- And . . .

The Fourth Tool for Life with Roommates: Fun

So, you know to speak up when you have to, you're good with the Thank-you's, and you're okay to scrub the shower when it gets dangerous. Now, for life with roommates to be the coolest, all you need to add is fun, and life with roommates can be the best time you've ever had.

You'll work hard, and you'll study hard, so in order to achieve a healthy balance in your life you'll have to play hard. You're obliged. So now that you have permission, party on! If you're the shy type, you will need to be led astray by the more adventuresome. If you're lucky, you may have a bad example to emulate right in your own apartment: You can make things memorable without even leaving home.

Many of your predecessors' tales are recounted with great respect and envy—stories about the tours the guys next door conducted of the drainpipe system under the street, for example. They charged five dollars a head and covered several city blocks. It was for a great cause; they were raising funds for a backyard distillery. They were so successful, they even considered lighting up part of a tunnel and renting it out, but one of the locals turned them in (a water inspector well past his adventure years).

Then there's the story about the all-night party with a twist. The address was elevator number three, hosted by apartment number 602 and it had everything: music, dancing, drinks, and Chee·tos. It was a surprise party and the guest of honor was anyone who entered that night. At dawn they unhooked the speakers, sent the strip-o-gram guy home, and hosed down the elevator.

Some pranks go too far and are barely discussed. Their whispered stories include words like "school expulsion," "history prof," and "vinyl." Embellishments are not discouraged.

A less crazy but equally inspired happening occurred on a great rainy weekend when the front yards on South Street became a sea of mud, perfect for staging the "South Street Olympics" with the neighboring student houses. The competitions included the Downhill Mud Roll, the Belly Mud Flop, and the Mud Discus Chuck, ending with the Great South Street Hose-Down. The homemade ribbons and medals will be cherished forever. People are already signing up for next year.

Those who came before you made the climb to fame with minimal property or liver damage. They suffered little heartbreakage and few failing grades. And most were able to crawl into work or write their exams.

It doesn't have to be crazy to be fun. There will be the equally memorable times of community cooking and hockey games on the television, of fixing each other's hair and each other's love affairs, of lending an ear, and sharing your last dollar.

Cherish this time!

Part 3

Feast and Famine: From "Fine Dining" to Food Banks— Striking a Balance

Chapter 11

Find a Map to Your Kitchen

So it's come to this: Since you've been on your own, you have every "We Deliver" joint on your speed-dial. You salivate when you see Styrofoam and you're rapidly heading for fast-food rehab. Your take-out habit is so bad that you're looking to pawn your lava lamp to finance your next Whopper. Now you're penniless and hungry and ready for *the cure*. Relax, for your salvation lies just beyond your pizza box burial ground. Move the bicycles and the iguana out of the kitchen and survey your new domain 'cause now you're cooking!

In no particular order, here are some ways to ensure a smooth debut as a chef.

1. Today, you ate your Cheerios out of a frying pan; face it, your kitchen is a pigsty. Crank the tunes and find the soap.
2. Will it kill you to think healthy? Get an official food guide from student health services or the public health office. (Forget the false nose. These people will not remember you.)
3. To turn groceries into food, connect with the Internet, your local library, and your relatives. Apply the KISS principle. (You know: Keep It Simple, Stupid.) Invest in a simple fast-meal cookbook.
4. You went out on your own with good intentions so you probably have something that resembles food in your fridge. Check it all carefully. Unless you're working on a microbiology project, the brown slime dish should go.
5. Food that wasn't green when you bought it shouldn't be green now; chuck it.
6. Fruit and veggies that are shriveled aren't bad; they're just, well . . . shriveled. You could turn the fruit into juice or salad and the vegetables into soup.
7. Best-before dates may be stretched just a bit. Use the sniff test.
8. Improperly cooked or handled raw meat can be seriously dangerous. No kidding! Cook meat ASAP or freeze after a day.

9. If you've ignored the above warning, one bout of food poisoning will convince you, should you survive.
10. Wash kitchen cloths often; smelly cloths are full of bacteria—yuck.
11. Oh, and one more thing: Wash your hands! (Did this have to be said?)

Chapter 12

Guided Tours of Your Supermarket: They Really Do Exist!

Picture yourself following a tour guide down the supermarket aisles; shoppers watching, thinking you're on a day pass! If you don't have the cojones to go it alone, a couple of your buddies could be dragged out there with you. In fact, your guide would be a nutrition expert and food shopping pro with good things to show you. (For an adventure, put an ad on a bulletin board at school or work and see who shows up for the tour with you.) This service exists in many stores. If you can't find one that provides it, a good store manager could arrange something for you. This may not exactly compare with touring, say, a music recording studio, but the information is of value for life.

Here's what one or two hours of possible embarrassment could get you:

Hungry minds need to know:

- What Constitutes Good Nutrition: See It Here First!
- Creating Balanced Meals: Shocking Formula Uncovered.
- Tips on Reading Food Labels: Secrets Revealed at Last.
- The Lowdown on Unit Pricing: The Truth Comes Out!

WHAT'S UNIT PRICING?

Q. If a five-pound box of soap costs $3.99, and a seven-pound box costs $5.79, which is the best value?

A. The five-pound box. The five-pound unit price, shown on a tag underneath the item, shows $.80 per pound. At this price the seven-pound box should be $5.60, not $5.79. The seven-pound unit price shows $.83 per pound. Don't be fooled, okay? No calculator needed!

Phone or drop by a major food store and see what they offer. Besides the tours, you may find:

- Cooking Classes Options: Be the First to Sign Up.
- Recipes: Get Your Copy Now; Avoid the Rush.
- Free Food Samples! Say No More.

Chapter 13

When the Money Runs Out Before the Month Does: No Green = No Groceries

Mamma said there'd be days like this . . .

Big miscalculation! You're running out of food and it's several days of starvation before payday, be it student loan, living allowance, or an actual wage. An advance is out of the question. You know; you've tried. The bridges you've burned are still smoldering (and straightening out that mess is for another time). It's bad enough stewing about your studies or your job without worrying about filling your gut, but it's a sure thing you're not alone. It shouldn't be difficult to set up a food-foraging system for pooling ideas and leftovers.

The Famine Prevention Plan

Some easy things you can do to keep the wolf from your door:

- Plan end-of-month potluck dinners with friends (include football games). Divvy up the leftovers.
- Connect with the city relatives (like you promised the folks you would). Prearrange meetings through your parents, if necessary, and go see if all the stories are true.
- Know the dates of all the church suppers you can volunteer at. They'll pile your plate high.
- Check which stores slash their meat prices on Saturday night. (They do this if they're closed on Sundays.)

- Ask bakeries about day-old bread. Include the bakery department of supermarkets.
- Talk to the produce manager, too. A wilted head of lettuce in the supermarket is still better than the rotten one in your fridge.

Stretch your food:

- Freeze your leftovers, all of them. They'll look mighty appetizing down the road.
- Freeze in one-person serving size. Use baggies, margarine containers, or even plastic grocery bags. Label everything with contents and dates.
- Freeze any baked goods that don't look moldy (bread, muffins, bagels, etc.) for future toasting or nuking.
- Too-ripe bananas = banana bread.
- Wrinkled apples = applesauce.
- Cook doubles; freeze the extra.
- Cook and freeze vegetables that are past their prime.

If Famine Hits

- Call any nearby friend who's ever eaten your food. It's simple: "Dude, you got anything to eat? I'm coming over."
- Crash free-food affairs (a hungry student shows no class):
  - Wedding receptions.
  - Company picnics.
  - College faculty functions (dedications, awards, staff recognition, retirements with "free refreshments," you're there).
- Visit those relatives, no matter how questionable the lineage. Uncle Jimmy's ex-wife's cousin might welcome you with a feast complete with leftovers, treats from her freezer, and return invitations. Return their generosity: Shovel their driveway, mow their lawn, etc.
- Pawn your treasures. Try not to be a regular at the local pawnshops and stash the ticket carefully for when you're back in your game again.

- Salvation Army, mission services, food banks:
  - All offer emergency food assistance. (You'll find food banks in many colleges and universities.)
  - They're in the phone book.
  - Won't they become your favorite charities when you're rich and famous!
  - Offer to work for your dinner.
  - Don't feel too bad; you'll be getting your act together soon. Make this a research project: You're immersing yourself in the subject matter.

Hey, you'll get a little scared, face a few hard times, and feel some humiliation. Big deal! There's an upside: You'll become a great problem solver, negotiator, deal maker, and social convener. And, of course, this would be the perfect time to scrub the fridge and cupboards now that they're totally empty . . .

Part 4

Budget Is Not a Four-Letter Word

Chapter 14

Your Basic, "Gotta-Do-It" Budget

How boring could it be to sit down and construct a budget?

Very, actually, but stick around, this won't take long.

Why budget, you may ask?

You budget in order to ensure that this task is not thrust upon you. Like when Mom has to pay your rent directly to the landlord and never lets you forget it. Or when your phone is now in Dad's name and the long-distance program has been removed from your

irresponsible grasp. Imagine that you're thirty-four years old with a spouse, two kids, and impending bankruptcy: The credit counseling bureau doles out your money till American Express no longer owns your sorry butt. That's why you learn to budget.

Cash flow crunches you'll want to avoid:
- Your prized possessions are regularly displayed in the pawnshop.
- Bumming money is losing you friends.
- Mold is becoming a condiment.
- You're scrounging for empties to sell.
- You leave lip marks on restaurant windows.

How to Make a Budget

All right, let's clarify a few things:
- You need to *not* blow one semester's student loan in the first two weeks of the school year.
- If you are working, you may be shocked by how much money is held back from your paychecks; you won't be getting the whole wad. You won't know for a while how much you spend on food or what the electricity will cost, so keep track for a few months.

Since most of your serious expenses are monthly ones, make it easier: Calculate monthly income against monthly expenses. Like so:

1. Write Down Income Sources

These could include:
- Student loans, bursaries, or scholarships (may be issued once per semester).
- Savings from summer jobs (must stretch from September to May—nine months).
- Living allowance from home (monthly?).
- Salaries from present jobs (every two weeks).
- Other (you should be so lucky).

2. *Calculate One Month's Supply of Cash*

Income	Amount and Time It Must Last	Amount per Month
Student loan/ bursary/scholarship	$1,200.00/September to December	$300.00
Summer job savings	$2,000.00/ September to June	$200.00
Allowance from home	$150.00/Month	$150.00
Salary	$90.00/Week	$360.00
Other: The Grandpa Connection?	$100.00/Month	$100.00
		$1,110.00 Total Monthly Income

3. *Figure Out One Month's Expenses*

- List *every* single expense for a month; include the movie rentals, shampoos, and jay-walking tickets.
- Figure out *when* you have to put out the cash, and
- *How* you pay it out. What could be easier?

Get yourself a freebie calendar and mark your historical dates.

Expenses	Due When	Amount	Amount/ Month	Paying How
Rent	1st of month	$450.00	$450.00	Give check to landlord.
Electricity	Once per two months	$90.00	$45.00	Mail check.
Telephone	15th of month	$38.00	$38.00	Mail check.
Bus Pass	1st of month	$50.00	$50.00	Pay cash.
Food	Weekly	$65.00	$260.00	Pay cash.
Savings	1st of month	$25.00	$25.00	Deposit to savings account.
Total Expenses/Month				**$868.00/ Month**

Oh joy! Your income is $1,110.00 a month and your expenses are $868.00, with $242.00 to spare! *Not so fast!* That's just eight bucks a day for that missing budget item called "miscellaneous." Shelter, food, and transport, that's easy. It's the incidentals, life's hidden surcharges, that sneak up on you: the badly needed haircut, the must-see movie, the lost bus pass, and the shoes that finally died. Add to that a cherished kitty that overdosed on some bad mouse and needs an after-hours clinic to make her better and what do you have? Real-life barfing all over your budget! Life happens. Does this sound like yours?

Monday: The old gang back home must be lonesome by now. Time for a marathon phone session with the meter ticking and a jumbo bill adding up.

Wednesday: What do you mean the cable bill didn't get paid? Top priority item here; isn't there football on TV this weekend?

Thursday: You've had it with waiting for the bus in the rain and hail an expensive cab to get you home.

Friday: You decide to get a life. That includes two clubs and a jazz bar = cover charge and the price of a drink or four.

And by *Saturday* morning, you're looking for a food bank!

Too much outgo, not enough income!

You haven't been flying solo for long, so what's a newbie to do? Your bid for independence has degenerated into late-night collect calls home for money.

Is this cash-flow problem temporary? If so, see chapter 13 on finding food. Will you be fine come payday or student loan payout day? Your boss might give you an advance on your next paycheck, or the student financial office could offer you some assistance.

Everybody runs out of money. What's your reason? Get a paper trail going and see how you really live.

Chapter 15

Since We're Talking Money, Let's Talk Taxes

It's a trick-or-treat world. For all the good stuff that will come your way—the amazing concert, the ultimate wave, and maybe the perfect date—crummy stuff will come along to work you over. Your car will croak, and you'll get canned. You'll probably get dumped; and, for sure, you will pay taxes.

Get a little perspective on your taxes: Because of them, there are loans to get you through school, parks to chuck Frisbees, and ice rinks to chase pucks, not to mention paved roads, fire departments, and street lights. Without taxes, you could be sitting in the dark, in the cold, with no juice for your stereo. Taxes are good . . . and tax rebates even better.

Now that you feel all warm and fuzzy about paying your taxes, you no doubt want to proceed. First, look up the deadline for your neck of the woods (it varies from country to country) so you'll know how long to procrastinate. Then, find the tax forms. The post office has them, the local revenue office has them, and you can download and print them off the Internet.

Doing It

Help is at hand!

- Your school's business/accounting students need the practice and their work is supervised by the profs. No charge or low charge.
- Community centers provide tax filing services for the low-of-income folks like seniors and students. If there's a charge, it's small or geared to income; it's worth checking out. Bring your student card.
- Tax companies (under "tax return preparation" in the yellow pages) have trained staff to prepare your tax return, usually while you wait/sweat, then e-file it for quick processing. Fees depend on the amount of papers involved (and the mess you bring). And they offer cash-backs. That's two fees you're paying: One to get your taxes done, and the second to put some moolah in your hand *now*. Think about it.
- The family money manager: Fill out your own papers (the working copy) and have them checked by Mom or Dad—whoever's been sweating over the tax forms for the last twenty years. (Don't get them started on that topic!) They know a thing or two about the subject.

Do-It-Yourself!

- The tax forms come with instructions (although research shows that these were developed by descendants of torturers). Your city has a tax office staffed with people who have been retrained and are now a kinder, gentler breed of government employee. You get a humanoid on the phone, ready to walk you through the murky parts. Do what you can before you call; there's a big population to service. If you end up owing money, discuss payment options with them. Ask for suggestions to avoid this in the future. (Consider bigger paycheck deductions or an investment account to make money for future tax payments. Yeah, right . . .)

- The tax preparation companies will double-check your figures for you. The fee is lower than if they did it all, but ask before you commit.
- Tax software: These programs are reasonably priced and more user-friendly than ever. You have the option of filling out your return, printing it, and snail-mailing it in or you can connect to the Internet and e-file it.

Get your papers together. (Papers? What papers?) Gather your receipts: employment, tuition, medical, school, or work expenses, etc. Learn what's deductible: your work clothes and tools, books, travel costs, etc. After hours of searching and many phone calls for replacement slips and tuition papers, you'll find a spot in your sock drawer for your receipts for next year.

Tax talk wouldn't be complete without a little slapping-around. You can P.O. a lot of people in your lifetime, but the tax man isn't one of them. It makes the feds unhappy when citizens cheat. The villain is routinely found and punished with big fines and home visits. Ever hear of Al Capone? A biggie in the Mafia, he was never charged for all the offings he masterminded, but was eventually convicted and imprisoned for, yes, tax evasion! To avert a life of felony, file your taxes, do it every year, and file before the deadline. And be forewarned that creativity is very much discouraged.

The deductions that aren't:

- Snowboarding lessons are not tax deductible unless they're part of the college curriculum.
- The cost of recreational pot is not yet a medical expense.
- Paying for theater tickets is not a charitable donation; the government doesn't care how bad the play was.

- Your body piercer is not a health care provider, no matter how many alcohol swabs she hands out.
- Getting a tattoo is not considered a medical procedure.
- Your cat, Bob, may not be claimed as a dependent.

Part 5

Navigating Bureaucracy: Changing Your Address Without Going Postal

Chapter 16

Your Friend the Civil Servant

So here you stand squirming while some official person sneers down on your application forms. (Screwed-up citizenship papers you think, or mortgage application at least; but no, just a simple change-of-address card.) You probably forgot something piddling like an apartment number. But wait—what if that sneer is actually a nasal twitch and your kindly postal clerk proceeds to look after you and send you on your way? It's possible.

What do civil servants, bureaucrats, and ticket agents have in common? They all have something you want. From birth certificates to school transcripts to the cheapest fare, your need is theirs to withhold or delay or complicate. While some see their role as the guardians of priceless treasures (these "treasures" being forms and files, and the record of your nineteen dollars savings account balance) and look upon you as nothing more than a festering rash, other officials remember what it is they're paid to do, and do it well.

You, the one with the need, aren't helpless in all of this. Don't just show up and get pushed around. Encounters with any sort of bureaucracy will get you what you came for because you're going in with a plan:

- Choose your time. Be there when they open (but not on Misery Mayhem Monday). Expect lines; don't go to the passport office when you're in a hurry. Rethink the noon-hour visit to a crowded city hall to whine about your parking tickets.
- Choose your attitude. Tomorrow is student loan pickup day; the school will be a zoo. Option one: Sigh, four hours wasted, hope you've got the right papers to claim your cash. Option two: Check your papers first, bring a book, and look spiffy. (Room jammed full of people = new friends, study partners, possibly a Friday night date . . .)
- Be in charge. You wear a smile, you make your request, and you are polite. If you fumble, so what? If you don't understand (bank jargon or tuition office babble), say that you're new at this, and ask for explanations. It's this easy: "Please explain!" You're in charge; you don't want to live your life always reacting to other people's behavior. Their job is to assist you. If you encounter jerks (and don't be overly sensitive), be in control: Keep smiling and stay polite.

  Service agencies, government and otherwise, employ many kind and helpful people, but it may not be your destiny to meet any of them. This is a sampling of those you may encounter:

- The Power Princess: Rude to the clients, rude to her staff, but will bow to any higher power; convince her that you're Bill Gates's cousin and watch her curtsy and kiss your ring; fun to watch.
- The Mental Pygmy: Knows nothing, can't help you; has memorized a few office policies, won't deviate from them; is related to the department head, will be promoted.
- The Sky Wart: Disgruntled airport worker; goal is to keep you separated from your flight for as long as possible, then bestow upon you the magic boarding pass and watch you scurry.
- Attila the Mom: Older, hair-in-a-bun, motherly looking, often found in faculty and school registration offices, has students like you for breakfast, chews them up and spits them out.
- Jilted Romeo: Dumped by someone you vaguely resemble; will reroute your paperwork through Alaska; abandon all hope.

If your goal is to make a nasty bureaucrat treat you better, forget it right now. It's not going to happen. Your satisfaction lies in getting what you came for and salvaging your day. Remember that old piece of advice:

No one can make you feel bad without your permission!

For the situations where repeat visits are necessary and you seem doomed to face the Evil One every time, amuse yourself with the following strategies:

Messing with Their Mind

To preserve your sanity, you've got to play little mind games: When you pretend you don't notice the acid dripping from their lips, when you smile brightly and thank them repeatedly for their trouble while contempt oozes from their pores, they figure that all is not right with you. They get confused. Their talents are wasted on you and you're no fun anymore. Suddenly your permit is stamped, your transcripts are ready, and you're out the door.

Borrowing Someone's Mother (Preferably Your Own)

Behind-the-counter bullies are surprisingly cooperative when a young person brings along a parent (or reasonable facsimile). Mothers and fathers become unhappy when anyone threatens their offspring and anything short of full, smiling service may be seen as a threat. The disgruntled guardian-of-the-files will sense this and back off. The aftereffects may last for one or two solo visits.

Biding Your Time

As no bad deed goes unrewarded, before too long these unpleasant people are eventually removed, no longer available to abuse a helpless public. Henceforth, they will reside in the inner offices, punished with a promotion and a raise.

In reality, bad behavior goes on because everyone lets it! If you get treated like dirt (whether or not your bank overdraft problem was dealt with, or the cable bill did get adjusted), immediately find a manager to speak to. If that *was* the manager who treated you like a lowlife, go up the chain of command till you get a listening ear. Do it while you're steamed or you'll lose your nerve. But act with composure and courtesy. There will likely be no public flogging of the offending party, but you'll feel better. A written complaint, polite and to the point, makes for good follow-up and provides a paper trail for ongoing problems (landlord hassles or unwarranted parking fines, etc.). This is all part of you taking charge.

You *will* experience the helpful and kind civil servant, someone only too pleased to guide you through the maze of bureaucracy and officialdom. This is the one whose name you remember and in whose line you patiently wait. And just as you made efforts to halt the harassment, it's even more important to celebrate the care and consideration of a good employee! Take that extra step. Your opinion counts. Find the boss, write a note (putting your praise in writing goes a long way toward spreading around some positive bureaucratic behavior), do the e-mail, go and tell. 'Cause you're in charge!

Chapter 17

The Telephone: Yours at Last!

It's amazing the number of people who run into trouble with their first telephone. There are so many attractive features available and it's the phone company's job to sell you on them, while not scaring you off by pointing out the costs. Watch how easy it is to slide into phone madness.

✦ ✦ ✦ ✦ ✦

The Rise and Fall of the Amateur Phone Owner

Step One: Signing Up

You stopped by the phone store to sign up and ordered the deluxe phone. All high-tech and speed-dial, it looks like the dashboard of a mini 747. You've seen them before—your parents have an early version—but this one has that special "Mine!" look. Bonus, the phone company offered all these neat extras to go with it. You don't have to pay the deposit up front; they'll put it on the phone bill, which is good (since it's almost half the rent).

Step Two: Becoming a Slave to the Call Features

All functions activated; you're good to go.

Check out these features:

- Shows who's calling: It's your parents' number; Mom checking in or checking up.
- Beeps while you're talking: Put your mom on hold; it's Kate with the latest on Mike; oops, forgot about Mom . . .
- Takes messages while you're talking: There's a beep while you're talking to Mike; no way are you putting Mike on hold; let the message program do its thing.
- Shows who's calling while you're on: talking to Mike again . . . and you're beeping; shouldn't really put him on hold; but wait, it's that hot guy Jordan on the display; Mike is so gone.

How could anyone live without these phone goodies? And each one costs only a few dollars a month!

Step Three: The Long-Distance Trap

Just a few long-distance calls: You don't know too many people around here yet. Give Lorie back home a quick call, and maybe Jason, to give them your new number. Almost forgot Kelly; she's a riot. But, boy, does she talk.

Step Four: Reality Bites

First month's bill: Whoa, that's huge! Not only the deposit but the forgotten hook-up charge, too. (Don't they just flip a switch?)

Step Five: No Relief in Sight

Second month's bill: Hold on. How many "fone-features" did you sign up for anyway? Plus the charges for those conference calls; are you closing corporate deals here? And from the amount of 411 calls (each call is almost a dollar), it looks like the phone book is still buried somewhere in your bedroom. And the beat goes on.

Step Six: Over the Edge

Third month's bill: No way! You can't pay this! And some agency keeps calling, sounding like they'll be sending Vito over to crush your kneecaps if you don't pay up by midnight!

And finally, as you wonder how you got yourself into this mess, the voice of reason reverberates inside your brain: "*Step away from the phone!*"

✦ ✦ ✦ ✦ ✦

It doesn't have to be this way. Where is it written that you have to do the screwing up to learn life's lessons? Let someone else wreak havoc on their lives. You can watch and learn.

Now, observe the wisdom of the telephone pro.

Avoid the Deposit Payment

When you're signing up for the first time, arrive at the phone office prepared. Some phone companies do not request a deposit from post–high school students. Bring along government ID (your Blockbuster card won't do). If you're a student, have proof of attendance. If you've been working, bring proof of employment and length of work time. If you can't get the deposit waived, note that after six months of paying on time and in full, it will be credited back to you on your bill. Rules and amounts differ, so find out.

Build Your Credit Rating

If you can carry this phone account thing under your own name and are a reliable bill payer, getting stuff like cars and houses will be easier down the road. If your phone is in a parent's name, you get no credit even if you're the one making the payments. Since students may be exempt from the deposit, see about removing your parent's name while you're still in school. Then, when you're out of school, the folks from the electric, gas, water, and phone companies will *not* be lining up demanding deposit money since you were building up a good credit history while you were still a student. You win.

Buy a Phone, Don't Rent from the Phone Company

Cancel the rental. (Did you know you were renting the phone? Don't feel bad, lots of people paid rent on a twenty-five dollar phone every month for eighteen years; imagine their excitement when they figured *that* out!) Buy a cheap, funky-looking phone at the discount store. (A red, plastic convertible? A blue beer can with a tinny ringing noise? Excellent, but keep the receipt close by, these goodies tend to have the shelf life of a cucumber.)

Kiss all the calling features goodbye. (It needn't be forever.) Stick with the bare bones phone plan (you *will* live). You can train yourself to not be owned by a telephone. There will be no more buzzing, beeping, or flashing; each caller will be a surprise. You'll learn how to handle telemarketers and you'll build character. If your line is busy, your friends will call back. Maybe you'll get an answering machine for Christmas.

Request a block on the long-distance/toll calls. Do it before you get roommates; this is one of the most effective steps you can take to avoid money conflicts over unclaimed phone bills.

Prepay your long-distance calls. Buy phone cards from a convenience store for your toll calls (good birthday present). Some are incredibly low-priced, at a penny a minute. Read the fine print about expiry dates. Program the access numbers into your phone; most cheap phones have number storage.

The cell phone: You could forget about the land-line phone and get a cell with a rock-bottom price—no disconnect or reconnect fees. But a cell phone package is unlikely to be cheaper than a basic land line. If a worried parent is paying for an emergency cell phone for you, know the deal and stay within the package limits. Don't take advantage of their concern. It's disheartening for parents when their kids are smart enough to get into college but have trouble tracking their phone time!

Remember your other communication options: e-mail, snail-mail, and that old standby, the face-to-face conversation.

The telephone is for *your* convenience: Don't let it run your show.

Chapter 18

The Overdue Bill: You *Will* Be Sorry!

There once was a man overloaded with bills who was being bothered by a collection agency. The agent was quite rude and so our man told him, "Mister, every month I put my bills in a hat and pick one out. That's the one I pay. I'm telling you, if you don't change your attitude, you won't be in next month's draw . . ."

Not many people are so laid back about their overdue bills piling up. And it's a good thing people worry or the economy would be in chaos. So if you're waking up more stressed than when you went to bed, if you're paying the Visa bill with your MasterCard and the only thing that comes out of your mouth when the phone rings now is: "Tell them I'm not here," then you might be in trouble.

You know you're in fiduciary hell when:

- You're studying by candlelight.
- Your car is back on the dealer's lot.
- Your most frequent visitor is the repo man (and now he's dating your roommate).
- Your landlord is starring in all of your nightmares.
- It's mealtime at your friends' place and yes, it's you at their door again.
- Good news: The collection agency for the cable company stopped calling. Bad news: It's because your phone's disconnected.

- Your folks, who've bailed you out a time or four, have switched to an unlisted number.

If any of these scenarios are familiar to you, a chat with a friendly credit counselor could help smooth things out. Check your school's financial services. (They know your story! Some of them have been there themselves.) Or look in the yellow pages under Credit Counseling, Family Services. They offer help with money management and mediation with creditors; they can also set up payment plans you can handle. Congratulate yourself for seeking help. It's a great relief to take control. Don't forget how embarrassed and scared you felt; this will help you stick with the plan.

Part 6

Building Your Own Safety Net: A Resource Kit

Chapter 19

The Buddy System: Forming Alliances

It's great to escape the homestead but it can be lonesome, too, and scary! It's what you want to do and this is where you want to be, but, man, who's got your back?

Organized "buddy systems" are now commonplace in many schools and workplaces. Buddying up is not just to keep you from being mugged or taken advantage of; it can provide you with some guidance and company. At school, there are selected peers to steer you through the maze of first-year college. Schools make great efforts to protect you from and educate you about stalking, harassment, and date rape. Campus-escort couples will walk you to and from night classes.

On the job front, employers are thinking hard about keeping good workers, and one common strategy is to provide mentors for career-minded staff. Educate yourself about all the tools out there, and then add your own. Build up a network of buddies; they'll help make this "on-your-own" gig sweet and smooth.

Buddies come from every walk of life, male or female, young or old. For example, Jonah was walking home from school one day when an old man tripped and fell in front of him. Jonah helped him up and recognized Mr. Losardo from the neighborhood. The man looked okay but accepted Jonah's offer to see him safely home. The conversation turned to school and how the math courses Jonah needed to graduate were killing him. The old man invited him into his house and showed him an office filled with books on architecture, physics, and math! "Maybe I can help," he said. Not only was Mr. Losardo a retired professor happy to help Jonah with his math, but he was also a master of pasta, Jonah's great love! Jonah became a regular who didn't just eat and learn: He tuned up his new friend's computer and kept his yard looking great. How's that for good encounters?

Why else would you need a buddy system (besides to keep from drowning in the pool at the "Y")? You want a buddy:

- When you have a perfect prank that needs a partner in crime.
- When, later, you need an alibi.
- When the alibi falls through and you need someone to share the blame.

You need a buddy because it's no fun to yell obscenities at football officials all by yourself or scream alone at a rock concert. And let's not forget that, when out on the town, most girls can't pee alone.

Seriously, though, buddies look out for each other, hide car keys, and bring hangover medicine. You'll pick up good buddies along the way. They could be your workmates, your roommates, or your classmates. The girl your age you see in the park every day walking her dog, for example. How about the guy that got dumped by the same girl who dumped you?

Things buddies do for each other:

- Buddies take turns staying sober.
- Buddies stay awake through the play-by-play of each disaster date.
- Buddies prevent the dreaded solo entrance into the campus pub.

- They tow each other's dead cars off the freeway.
- Buddies forage for food together.
- Buddies post bail for each other (during your activist stage, and your pal's pub phase).

Understand that a buddy system is a two-way street. When you're there for the two A.M. postmortem of your friend's latest breakup, she'll be there on your moving day. When your evicted classmate needs your couch for the weekend, he'll be the one driving you to the airport for your next visit home. The friend that puked on your shoes may be just the one to recruit when your place needs wallpapering. Don't be a taker, but don't be a doormat. Find the balance.

Chapter 20

Barter: A Resource for Every Millennium

Currency for the Cashless

Bartering is another nifty tool you can add to your survival kit. This exchange of goods or services has been valued for centuries. Hunters exchanged their pelts and meat for grain, cloths, and spices. And someone probably paid for your grandpa's birth with a pig and some fat hens dropped off at the doc's back door.

Guess what? Many international corporations practice the ancient art of barter today! There are newsletters and Web sites and even organized barter clubs. And what do all these businesses have that you don't? Nothing! Everyone has bargaining power. A hotel owner trades the use of a few empty luxury rooms for a fancy photocopier. A restauranteur trades excellent tables for a high-priced accountant's time. An artist pays for her family's haircuts with her beautiful pottery, and a student tutors the landlord's kid for a cut in the rent.

This is how bartering enters your life: The cupboard is bare, save for the six cans of tuna left from the case sent in last fall's care package. It's not that you don't like tuna but as a breakfast dish it's lost its appeal. Your roommate has been on a strict Rice Krispies diet, her shelves stocked with cereal and little else. When you both figure out that these are not the latest weight-loss fads, pride gets tossed aside and someone says: "Wanna trade?"

The hardest thing about bartering is starting. Going it alone is a drag; rejection is a pain. Establish your cronie connections, then force the subject out into the open and you're on! Be very clear—no one is bumming anything. You have marketable talents and goodies: you're the best essay writer on the continent; you have a life supply of *the* primo popcorn (it's just that you're out of absolutely everything else).

It gets easier after that. Roommates start going through their food, CDs, and other valuables to see what they can put "on the exchange." It's important to have a semblance of equal value. Get a handle on what things cost so you won't be the dweeb who offers a can of beans for the T-bone in your buddy's freezer.

Bartering is not for wimps. Imagine a meeting with your landlord, Walter, "the Wall," a gloomy, unapproachable fellow whose hobbies include intimidating tenants and sidestepping repairs. Knowing he's a tightwad, you and your housemates show him your plan to shape up the front porch in return for a month's rent. He doesn't slam the door on you; he knows the house is an eyesore. If it looks better, he can squeeze more rent out of *next* years' students. Two of you were helpers on a construction site for a summer (never mind why you got the boot; you've outgrown your clumsiness), plus, your uncle, the contractor, will get the materials at cost. Walter's in! (Get the deal in writing!)

Landlords have many needs that one as wonderful and talented as you can attend to in return for low or *no* rent. Look for:

- Broken down cars that your magic fingers can heal over a few weekends.
- Computers that double as door jambs till you transform them into cyber-marvels.
- Offspring who can't grasp calculus till you step in.

Rules

1. Do your best work!
2. The service you provide can't eat up all your time.
3. The done job must not fall apart.

Consider a mini contract for your "service-for-rent" arrangement so no one gets ripped off:

We, Tom, Dick, and Harry, agree to paint the exterior of the house (15 Glendale Drive) in return for the next (May) month's rent at same house. We agree to the following:

- *Paint will be on the house, not windows, bushes, or driveway.*
- *Volume of work music will be reasonable.*
- *Thorough cleanup.*
- *Work ready for inspection and finished before May 1.*
- *No rent receipts for May (since no money exchanged hands).*

Signed this day, etc., by etc.

I, Mary, agree to offer May's rent in return for the exterior painting of the house at 15 Glendale Drive. I agree to:

- *Supply the paint and work supplies (including ladders, tarps, brushes, and brush cleaners).*
- *Inspect and allow for corrections before May 1.*

Signed this day, etc., by etc.

Once you've bartered your way out of a few shelter and food dilemmas, and the prospect of sleeping *and* eating in a Dumpster has not materialized, then you might see the art of barter as more than just for emergencies. The ideal barter scene? The one where the world now comes to you: The phone rings; it's Nicolas from down the hall. "Hey, I'm outta food, but I've got toothpaste, a movie pass, and thirty minutes left on my phone card. Whatcha got?"

Chapter 21

Community Service: Giving a Little Back

First thing that comes to mind is jail time, right? A few guys get Saturday-night stupid in the Lonesome Saloon parking lot and it lands them a date with the judge, a big fine, and two hundred hours of community service. No, no. This is about noticing that the world out there could use a little help, and that you, with all your energy and your cool, are well equipped to lend a hand.

You had a little attack of conscience watching the neighbors out in full force (minus you) for "Clean Up Our Park" day. Did some of the garbage look familiar? So you're thinking of doing a bit of volunteer work in your community, donating to the cause. 'Cause this could be where boy meets girl! (And worker meets CEO . . .)

Wait! Between catching up on missed classes and your full life as a sports fan, how will you find time to be a "contributing member of society"? Just fixing your hair takes half a morning; when are you going to find time to save the world? And will it interfere with pub night?

Actually you can provide invaluable services to humanity in small chunks of time:

- You can recycle.
- You can donate blood.
- You can sign your donor card (the ultimate in recycling!).

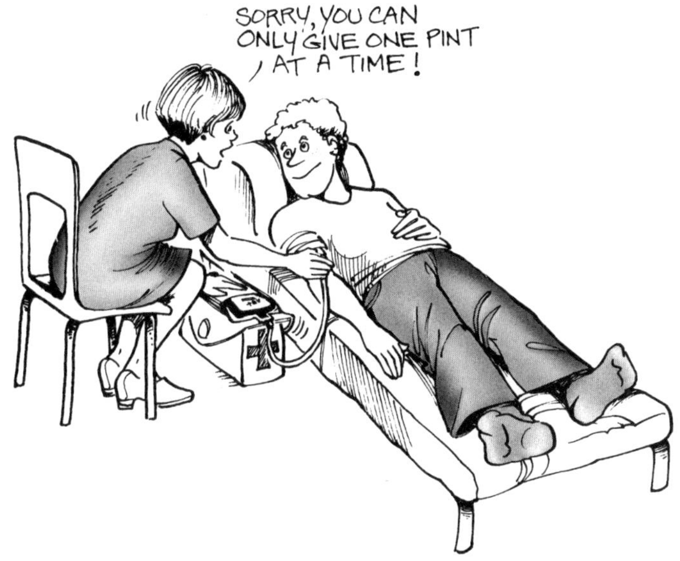

Some activities need more time and commitment, such as joining a neighborhood watch, lobbying for more buses, or running for town council. Community fund-raisers such as Terry Fox Runs and Mother's Day telethons will happily use you for the whole year's prep time or just for the day itself. These organizers are smart, resourceful people. Usually well connected, they could represent many opportunities for you down the road. Get to know them.

Other projects will require some training. And sometimes a police check, if you're to assist vulnerable people. (Relax. The teen helpline workers don't really care about your parking violations and your pathetic grad night in the drunk tank. Police checks are about flushing out abusers and con artists.)

Use your passions. Apply to be on the community editorial board of the local papers to share your opinions with the world. If you're radical—if you like to express yourself while chained to the dean's desk, body weakened by hunger strikes—then the school newspaper should welcome you with open arms.

Feed the homeless. If you've ever needed a soup kitchen in the past, seeing both sides of the ladle gives you perspective. That good ol' "been there" feeling is priceless.

You have to keep safe. Phoning lonely shut-ins for a nightly chit-chat is safe. Taking inner-city kids to the bowling alley on Saturday mornings is relatively safe. (Some of those seven-year-olds are brutal.) Heading into the city's combat zone for the clean needle exchange isn't.

You should be having fun. Check with your school. Do they have annual bed races to help buy incubators for sick babies? Do they have car washes (usually boisterous, well-attended affairs with food and music) to raise cash for playgrounds? Young people don't always enjoy a good rep with the rest of the community. College students are seen as transients who wreak havoc and then pull out. So, when kids are seen giving their time and energy to their host communities, the locals provide enthusiastic support. Give it a shot.

You've got to get satisfaction. Some of your volunteer jobs will be eye-openers and make you grateful for your life. Most can find their way into your résumé. Some are boring—and you should move on to more pleasing projects. Others will make you feel so good that you'll forget that your original goal was to go out and get lucky!

So, from de-icing the sidewalk in front of your building to joining peace rallies, you'll change the world. Young people like you have sponsored devastated refugee families. They've run for cancer research and unbeached whales. Never feel powerless. You have clout. Call up the community center or dial city hall and tell them you're coming!

Chapter 22

Transportation: Wheels or Heels—How Are You Fixed?

So you've got your own place *and* you've got yourself a set of wheels. You're living large! If your ride is the result of many work hours and disciplined savings, pat yourself on the back. (If the bank stills owns a chunk of it, picture a "Paid in Full" letter on your fridge door before too many moons.) If you've inherited a family car, even if it's the old beater, be grateful. Be very grateful!

Get familiar with the insurance details. Whether you're under the family coverage or your own, find out about the policy conditions such as who may drive the car besides you. Forget the "Oh, it's cool, I'm covered" mindset. In case of an accident, even a minor one, ask yourself: 1) Will the insurance rates quadruple? and 2) How upset will your parents be? If it's your parents' coverage, will your car be in permanent lockdown? If it's *your* policy, where will you store your now uninsured and useless car? Know the deal.

Now be real. Are you going to run it into the ground till you have to sell the stereo to pay someone to drag it to the car cemetery? Or do you think you can remember to protect it from the likes of you? If you keep your vehicle looking great and running smooth, such questions are insulting. The mechanically challenged will come crawling to you for advice. Will you be there for them?

When it comes to finding car help, go visit the guy down the street whose car appears well loved. Ask him where to take yours and if you may use his name: "Steve sent me; he said to ask for Mario." Referrals provide a bit of security for you.

If a college or high school nearby has an automotive department, they may need your junker almost as much as you need them! Bonus! (Prepare to be rejected. Don't take it personally.)

If you have to find yourself a mechanic on your own, be aware that, as in any profession, there are good ones, great ones, incompetents, and scammers. While your car is still well (you think), take it for a "lube-oil-filter" service; generally a $20 to $40 deal. This includes a multiple point inspection. The mechanic may find some legitimate problems that may cost lots to fix. If he or she doesn't inspire confidence, take your car elsewhere and ask for a diagnosis from another mechanic. If you're getting differing sets of problems, you've become someone's make-work project. But whose? Call the Better Business Bureau to ask about complaints on any of them. Proceed from there. Get estimates, ask around. It may well be that your car's future performance is going to pick your mechanic for you.

You know how expensive it is to support a car. There's your gas, insurance, maintenance, repairs, plate tags, and emission-control checkups. Then factor in parking tickets, speeding tickets, and the fines for assorted violations, like the broken taillight you got in that tussle with the fire hydrant. You "forgot" to get it fixed, the cop noticed and tagged it on to your speeding ticket, and you're faced with this burning question: If you have a car, will you have to live in it?

A car is a lethal weapon, and a very expensive one at that. It's also a Dumpster, a sound booth, a store room, a commuter train, and a motel. It's been a source of concern for your parents since you started driving and their worry doesn't end now that you're leaving. In fact, their anxiety level has ratcheted up and you'll be served up some familiar refried warnings. They want you safe and they want you responsible. Give them the courtesy of your listening ear. Understand where they're coming from.

"Best of . . ." Naggings from Parents, Inc.

"For now, the car has to get you from A to B. Worry about getting the 'Babe Magnet' when you get the bucks." Relax, you're not a high school kid anymore; you know that your beater car shouldn't be an obstacle to your love life. And anyone who objects to your wreck is better left at the curb.

"I can't believe you're buying faux fur seat covers, woofers, amps, and fancy rims while we subsidize your education!" See, now that's why you support yourself. You can tart up your wheels any way you want when you're the one who's financing.

"Do you really think your idea of mirror ornaments is tasteful?" Folks don't get that it takes much research to select just the right dashboard decor. If it's a family loaner, all dancing skeletons and fad-of-the-month accessories are removed the instant the car touches the home driveway. No stickers that can't unstick if the car's not yours. Bonus if your parents think it's a hoot to drive their "college-kid's-home-for-the-weekend-can-you-believe-this" car!

"Before you come home, clean out all the fast food trash on the floor and wash the car once in a while. 'Wash me' carved in the grime is not impressive." In fact, some kids schedule a visit home as motivation to hose down (and out) their mobile swamp. That's when you find the lost physics book and the overdue (sixty-three days) video . . . plus four dollars and thirty-nine cents in change and some unfamiliar underwear. Do you want your kid sister to clean out the car when you visit home? Or your mom?

"We helped you get the wheels, paid for insurance, and kicked in for repairs; the least you can do is find a small part-time job to keep gas in the tank." It should be a given that you're gassing up the car on your own dime. If the pressure's on strong but your cash is tied up in rent and food, consider a bus pass and long-term parking for the car. Once you're supporting yourself, start a car fund and get your own. Freedom is great but it's far from free!

"Get the car equipped with the necessities—first-aid kit, flashlight, blanket, candles and matches, shovel, jumper cables, etc." Great idea! Could be a birthday or Christmas present. Or a right-now care package.

"The car is not meant to pile six kids in and track three thousand miles down to Florida for the spring break. It's not good for the car!" Of course, the car is the least of their concerns. You know the real fears: Will you get robbed, beaten, raped; will you make it home alive? Parents have every reason to be upset. And the milder worries: Will you get drunk and wild and bad? They probably have vivid memories of their own hair-raising adventures tearing down the highway toward a beer-soaked beach. Ask them all about it.

"Cell phone usage, talking, eating, and sex are to be indulged in while vehicle is in a stationary mode." Weren't you told, growing up, to focus on the task at hand? Well then, pull over and enjoy what you're doing.

If you don't have a car, catching the bus or riding the rails has its pluses. Besides saving on car costs, you'll have opportunities for some great people watching, as well as people meeting. Bus stop regulars can become neat seatmates: people just like you with whom you feel a rapport, and people so different that it's an education just stepping onto the bus with them. People whose stories are so neat that you find yourself looking forward to tomorrow's installments, whether the conversations are directed to you or not (eavesdropping is definitely allowed), from the traveling pack of cleaning staff of a local hotel sharing juicy tidbits from their night shift to the fascinating old regular who has animated discussions with his companion, an invisible being apparently perched on the ceiling of the bus. (His fellow passengers don't blink an eye, a tacit tolerance of his quirkiness.) You'll see how babies smiling for strangers can change their whole demeanor, and how the bellowing and shoving of rowdy kids can cement the bad rep of all teens. Want to feel good in the bus? Give up your seat! (Small proof that today's young people can be plenty considerate.)

You can read on the bus, you can listen to your music (and keep it for your ears only), or you can study. Let's face it: You can't study while walking, and you shouldn't study while driving. Many a good test mark is directly related to the frantic study time in the back of the bus.

Remember to ask if a bus pass is built into your tuition fees. Check your local transit for monthly passes or student discounts.

Many schools and workplaces have ride boards for carpooling. If friends are driving you around, don't be a freeloader: If you don't provide the wheels, you provide cash for the gas.

Or, you could run, bike, in-line skate, or even walk. Does this make you a loser who can't spring for a set of wheels? No, actually, this could make you an athlete! Maybe last week you saw two long miles of hard sidewalk between you and your destination; today you're "in training!"—getting in shape, pushing some oxygen to your brain. Tomorrow may introduce you to hiker groups, running clubs, marathons, triathlons, who knows? All this because you had to leave the family car back home with the folks. You left home without a ride; and now you're turning rides down!

Wherever you go, make sure that getting there is a good time.

Part 7:

R&R: Do You Know How to Rock 'n' Roll? Being Your Own Social Director

Chapter 23

Kicking Back in a Strange Town

The weekend is coming and two questions are tops in your mind: What do you do and who do you do it with? (So far you've met a janitor and the pizza guy.)

Much as you want to party, when you're new in town it takes an effort to hurl yourself into the cruel, cold Saturday night. It's easy to give up on getting a social life and keep your ongoing date with the couch and the movie channel. But you can stay home when you're twenty-eight and old!

The trick is to follow the buzz to where the action is, find people who are going there, and go along with them. Students are bombarded with activities and people to play with, but you don't have to be a student to partake. Also, students don't have to restrict themselves to campus—get out and about.

Cities and schools have free weekly entertainment newspapers available in many locations, including variety stores, campuses, and newsstands. These papers are written by people of your generation so you're bound to find something good—and it needn't cost a wad for a night on the town since lots of great places are geared to penniless youth. Regular promotions push cheap beer and loud music: a winning combo!

Underage? For those of you who are not equipped with your own, legal drinking age ID, not everything has to be done with beer in hand. There are many campus and town activities that are a blast—and boozeless. Information is everywhere, you can find it.

Legal or underage, you're into more than just chugging beer! There's live music, DJs, dancing, and shooting pool. There are symphonies and chamber music concerts. Don't forget gyms, bowling, swimming, and organized sports. You can find community theaters, most of which would love to have you volunteer, help build sets, or star in the play. There are many ways to party! It won't be long before you'll be able to contribute your own answers to conversations that begin with, "So, what should we do tonight?"

No one likes to go out alone so how do you find someone to go with? When you're surrounded by students, it's easy enough. Someone calls out, "Going to (insert hangout name here) tonight; meet everyone at nine." And you're in! Get some details on location and dress code and go party. If no one is getting the ball rolling, what's stopping you? Fire up something yourself! You're shy? Worried about looking dumb? What if no one shows up? (Everyone secretly feels this way.) Take a chance. You could "what if" yourself to your couch forever. (Commit one or two classmates to travel with you.)

Unless you work in a tollbooth, you have coworkers who could be your ticket to a good time. Consult them about their weekends. Chances are they'll ask you along to their hot spots and you can size things up for yourself.

It's your town now but the turf isn't familiar yet so let's review the safety rules:

- Set up your ride home *before* you leave home.
- Don't drink your cab fare.

- Check if taxi drivers will come into the bar to fetch you.
- Date-rape drugs are not a passing fad: Never leave your drink unattended.
- If the bar bathroom looks like a pharmaceutical convention, move on.
- If the cops are already there as you arrive, move on.
- Bouncers and bartenders are good at diffusing trouble, and some will see you to your car or bus stop.
- Check out the campus escort system, whether you're male or female.
- The mildest of drinkers can morph into raging idiots when cut off booze; steer clear.

Later, when your buddy system is fully geared up, you can lower your guard and get cocky again.

Avoid specialty bars:

- Where the ladies love company but charge user fees.
- Where the doorman sells happiness in pill form.
- Where they don't just lock up the establishment at closing time; they roll armor down over it.

And now some brutal words:

- Humans plus beer equals good times; humans plus lots of beer equals stupidity.
- Being the drunken life of the party gets really old, really fast.
- Being called a "party favor" is not a compliment.
- Do you know when your last call is?

Factoid: When a bartender cuts you off, he or she is not out to embarrass you, shred your dignity, or ruin your life. This is just done to save the bar license and also to protect your sorry butt. So the words "You're cut off!" should not trigger a barwide brawl and mass destruction. You'll then get to spend your weekend in jail where someone bigger will slap you around and someone drunker will throw up on you. Word gets around and people won't go out with you anymore (which is fine since your life savings, student loan, and future earnings would all be earmarked for payment of fines and bar reconstruction). Are you having fun yet?

Look after yourself and party on!

You want to have the kind of time that, when you wake up sometime Sunday, man, you're smiling!

Chapter 24

Homemade Vacations: Too Broke to Break?

Call it spring break, school break, or study week: It's happening and everyone's going away but you. It seems that everyone you know has ski-lift passes and airplane tickets. Money is tight this year and you won't be flying to any wild, sandy beach. In your sad little mind, the whole world will be having a great time but you. The first thing to do is to feel sorry for yourself and get that out of the way. Then, think about having an unforgettable stay-at-home vacation!

What to Do

An excellent homegrown break begins with some prep time. Check out the ideas below. Lots of the info can be found in newspapers, tourist centers, and the yellow pages. Easier still, most of the events are listed on the Internet. If you don't have access to the Web, check the library computer department. Likely all that's needed for some Web time is a reservation and some ID. Not fluent in World Wide Web–ese? The staff will be happy to help.

What to Get

Borrow any or all of the following items from departing classmates, friends, and neighbors: DVD player and VCR (with movie discs and tapes), any sports or exercise equipment you might like to try, CD collections, health club memberships, any sports or concert tickets left unused, and a bus pass. Or, of course, if a good buddy's place includes most of the above toys, then borrow the whole apartment! (Stay worthy of your friend's trust; also, do a big cleanup before you leave.)

Do-It-Yourself Vacations

Sports Vacations: You the Fan

Attend as many sports events as your little heart desires. It may be spring break week but hockey still happens. Witness the awesome carnage of local amateur wrestling; thrill to the prowess of champion bowlers. If you love it and it's in season, you can find it. Become one with the TV sports channel, the speed channel, or why not the fishing channel? By all means, when requests pour in for your cat/plant/house-sitting services, check if a big-screen TV and pay-per-view are part of the deal.

Sports Vacations: You the Player

Get out and play with the toys you borrowed! Just remember: You break it, you buy new upgraded state-of-the-art replacement.

Film Fest

What's playing? Chances are that great old movies are showing somewhere. Find the film club in your city (there will be one) and see what's on.

Home Film Festival

Now you have the time to roam the aisles of the video stores and pick up cheap old thrillers. Don't forget that intriguing new movie that none of your friends wanted to see. Now you're free to view it unapologetically alone.

Live Theater

Double-check sold-out performances; they could still have single seats. Ask about dress rehearsals; they're usually free. (An audience is always good to have around.) And don't underestimate amateur productions. They're often as good as the pros'.

Get-in-Shape Week (Why Not?)

Yes, "Just do it." Try out the borrowed equipment. Venture into the Y. Dog-sit; walking your temp poochie will force you to move your body and provide a great excuse to talk to people (doggie = babe magnet on a leash). Maybe you own membership in your school phys-ed complex and didn't even know it. Go see.

Expand Your Food Horizons

What eateries does your town have to offer? It's cool to dine alone; if you don't feel that way, bring a book. (This tip from an actual health inspector: Visit the bathroom; if the can is clean, so is the kitchen!) Check the food section of the papers, the restaurant guides, or the Internet for exotic food venues. Actually, why not check supermarket aisles where you've never ventured before. Be brave and cook something different. Hey, be brave and cook *anything*! You're both the guest and the guinea pig.

Be a Tourist

Take a guided bus tour of your city. Yes, you may be flanked by fogies; enjoy it and let them fuss over you. Or map out your own tour. Explore music stores, video arcades, martial art dojos, English pubs, and cemeteries. Hey, you know what stokes your coals. The city hall or the chamber of commerce can supply you with info on what's hot, what's cool, what's free.

More, More

- Import a friend/sibling (sibling must come weighed down with home cooking and leave with own dirty laundry). Take import for a tour of the city. Banish them home before the week's end so you can relish some veg time.
- Try an actual reading week. Find a library and help yourself.
- Learn neat stuff: How about medieval swordplay? Or a crash course in swimming, knitting, or skating. Look for a race car driving school!
- Investigate these possibilities:
  1. A one-week "first week free" membership at a health club.
  2. Job shadow at your dream corporation.
  3. Volunteering (often includes meals).

Secrets to keep from your friends:

- Here's an adventure: devout metal head? Go to the ballet.
- Rapper? Check out *Madame Butterfly* (that's an opera).
- And you classical music devotees: Check out the latest boy band.

Believe this: If you decide to have a good time, you will. Guaranteed.

Part 8

Your Health: Invincible Though You May Be . . .

Chapter 25

Is There Any Actual Medicine in Your Medicine Cabinet?

Oops! Breaking in new boots on a three-hour hike to Webster's Peak was not the best idea, and now you're home with two blistered feet in a pail of water.

Or maybe you've got the beginnings of a cold, which you hope will disappear overnight, but you greet the dawn with an aching throat, stuffy nose, and assorted grievances. How about the memorable "Please let me die!" character-building hangovers?

You want to have some relief available in your place, right now. No one wants to truck downtown to the pharmacy in the throes of nausea. So let's check out your medicine cabinet. Unofficial surveys report the following list of contents:

- Nothing at all, for those souls who didn't know that the bathroom mirror is also the door to the medicine cabinet.
- Used razor blades, stashed and used again, much to one's regret.
- Old, "spare" toothbrush, for when you drop your present one in the toilet.
- Skin-care products in glass jars that smash in the sink while you're digging for aspirin that's not there.
- Forgotten "objects" that will get you in hot water when your next true love arrives.

But no actual medicine! (That expired bottle of antibiotics you didn't finish like you were supposed to doesn't count, and shouldn't be stored in the bathroom anyway.)

So what *should* be in your cabinet? Some items, by their mere presence, will ward off their targeted ailments like a voodoo charm. Few burns or cuts will be visited upon your household after the purchase of a first-aid kit. And it is unlikely that you will have a fever if you actually own a thermometer.

Your basic medicine cabinet necessities:

- Headache and pain pills
- Throat lozenges
- Nausea medication
- Diarrhea medication
- Small first-aid kit with thermometer, bandages, and disinfectant
- Your particular sports injury relief (includes a bag of frozen peas labeled "Not for cooking!" stored in the freezer)

Bring your list to the pharmacy and find the expert in the back of the store. That would be your neighborhood pharmacist; she's the pro and is there to help you. Really! (More info, sometimes, than from your doc!)

Chapter 26

Be Well Now, Feel Great Later

Steps to keep you boogying into old age:

- Eat well. Amazingly, some of the food you like might actually be good for you.
- Move your body. Anything that gets your heart pumped is perfect. Walk, run, hike, dance. (Chewing and lifting the remote are not considered exercise.)
- Put music in your life. It does soothe the soul. And anything that's good for the soul is good for the rest of you.

- Rest. A candle that's lit at both ends gets the big meltdown. Your tired body doesn't heal, can't learn, and won't work. And, most importantly, a tired body can't play.
- Take control of what you can. Lose destructive relationships. Reconsider a dead-end job.
- Give; the payback is enormous. Rake your neighbors' leaves; give your single-mom friend the night off. Never mind that volunteering will "look good on your résumé," do it for yourself!
- Express yourself. Play a musical instrument. Rebuild an engine. Plant a garden.
- Don't keep things inside. Got problems? Get them out! If you can't talk 'em out, write them down. An $8^1/_2$ x 11 inch piece of paper will put your list of hassles into better perspective than letting them rattle around inside your head.

Chapter 27

Depression: It *Can* Get You and You *Can* Fight Back

Everybody feels sad sometimes. This new life of yours is exciting, but change can also bring stress and fear and loneliness. These feelings are normal and don't usually last long. Actually recognizing these feelings is a healthy thing: You become more aware of who you are and what you need, and you sharpen your coping skills. Although living on your own is bound to take you on some shaky rides, you'll come away with more strength and confidence than you had getting onto this roller coaster. Count on those not-so-fun times when your roommate leaves you rentless to go live with her boyfriend and your computer eats your five-thousand–word essay. You get over that shat-upon feeling. The girl next door will fish your school paper out of the bowels of cyberspace and you'll get thankful that it wasn't *your* boyfriend your roommate took off with. All of this just makes you stronger.

But when it seems that life sucks, day and night, with no sweetness in sight, and you have no real reason for feeling this way, then you could be suffering from depression, and you could maybe use a little help. When you can't remember when you last smiled, then it's time to get yourself looked after.

You know you're depressed when:

- Your energy level has tanked. The old guy next door takes half a day to wheeze past your house, but you can't even make it off the couch. Your "get-up-and-go" got up and went.

- Your latest hobby is extreme sleeping. You wake up for a pit stop and a bowl of cereal, then head back to bed.
- Or . . . you have no need for your alarm clock since you don't sleep anymore; you're the latest member of the one to six A.M. infomercial fan club, Insomniacs, Inc. It's a good thing you have no energy. If you could dial the phone, you'd be the bankrupt casualty of every scam on the tube.
- Nothing's fun anymore—not your friends, not the NBA, and not you. The Lakers win, who cares; your dream date finally calls, so what; your whole outlook on life: "Whatever."

- Your mom's care packages (so delicious that you used to charge your roommates just to sniff them) mean nothing anymore. You've stopped eating.
- Or, you stress-eat your way through the fridge, the cupboards, your roommates' food, and next month's budget. And it's not even fun.
- You know you're depressed when it takes you several tries to figure out that this sentence is about your inability to concentrate . . .

- You know you're depressed if you think the world would be a better place without you in it; when the words in your head say that life is the problem, and death is the answer. And you're buying it.

These are all symptoms of depression. But no one has to feel this way. Mental health advisers pretty much agree that suffering from more than half of these signs for several weeks indicates depression. It is crucial to see a doctor if you see yourself here. Sadly, our society is not as open to emotional challenges as we are to physical ones. We rush to get a broken leg fixed but we let our depressed mind go untreated. It's not right. Here are the "You know you're depressed when" symptoms listed again in more official terms. Do any of them sound familiar?

(Drug or alcohol abuse or grief caused by great loss can also cause these symptoms.)

If you recognize yourself here but can't get it together enough to discuss it, bring this list with you to the doctor and tell her, "This is me." And let them take it from there. Or, show the list to the kind of friend who will then walk you toward some helping hands.

If it's someone near to you who appears to be suffering from most of these soul-draining symptoms, offer some assistance: "You seem down lately, can I help?" Understanding and help work far better than "Snap out of it!" The telephone book has numbers for distress lines or advice on how to help someone else. Depression is not a fault, it's a fact! It's nothing to apologize for or be embarrassed by.

There is no reason for anyone of any age to suffer from depression. Today's treatments are very effective and can bring back that great kick-ass feeling again. You owe it to yourself and you're definitely worth it.

Part 9

You, the Worker

Chapter 28

Bosses, Colleagues, and Other Pieces of Work

New job? Then, It's Showtime!

- Show up—all of you, mind and body! Give it everything you've got, whether you're cutting grass or cutting diamonds.
- Show up on time. Staying late doesn't make up for it; that's just the way it is.
- Show respect for the pros; taking down the "new kid" is in their job description and you'd like them to go easy on you.
- Show your smart side. Do your homework. Arrive informed. (That doesn't mean you're cocky; just don't dumb down.)
- Show you care. Cool doesn't equal cold.
- Show yourself a good time. It's just a job. Learn to do it well and relax.

Jobs: The Good, the Bad, and the Ugly

The Good

You're glad to come to work and your coworkers are glad to see you. Because of you, customers are well looked after; because of you, patients feel better, students are inspired. You have a good boss who allows you some control and values the work you do. You've got the best a job can offer: satisfaction. Did you know that on the list of things that make people happy at work, the paycheck is *not* number one? Money is actually way lower than pleasant surroundings and challenging work. Job satisfaction tops the list! People will work terrible hours in a damp rat hole at a job they love.

You could walk into a job that makes you feel that way, or you could take a so-so position and make it good.

Pumping up the job:

- Ask for feedback; then act on it. Be in charge of getting as good as you can be.
- Find a mentor: someone experienced and confident to "watch you grow and let you go," to show you the ropes and help map out your future, a move that could turn a job into a career.
- Make yourself a plan. What do you want in your work future?
- Investigate continuing education. Explore "learn while you earn" options. Does the company offer paid course incentives?
- Check out other departments; learn how they're relevant to your department. This shows you the big picture and maybe shows you your next move.
- Document your progress, accomplishments, and education: You might have to blow your own horn.
- Is it okay to jazz up your work space? Music, pictures, fun stuff make you feel good and work better. You spend lots of time at work, so make the most of it.

Surefire career busters:

- Make random appearances at work
- Crawl in hungover more than once
- Be confrontational with the boss
- Rag on him in front of *his* boss
- Throw tantrums
- Make your personal problems front and center
- Be a bare-belly kid in a button-up office

The Bad

Some jobs just keep you down. You can't go up, you can't go sideways. The leaders can't lead and the workers won't follow. Sometimes, it's a dream job with a nightmare boss. Or, maybe the job is fine, but you've given it lots of time and the two of you just don't fit. And, these days, the buzzword is layoffs, and guess who's at the bottom of the totem pole? Well, the perfect time to dig up a new job is while you *have* a job! The rent is covered, you're stockpiling macaroni and cheese, and the pressure is low.

While loyalty to your workplace is a valuable trait, and job hopping makes you look like a risky prospect, don't let that glue you to the wrong job. Start by looking outside your own work-pod. You could find a wonderful new occupation just down the hall. Pick people's brains: You might need night or weekend courses for your future position, while you plug away at your entry position. You have a goal, a résumé, and a plan? You're good to go.

Loser philosophies for the workplace:

- That's not my job.
- That's not how we did it where I worked before.
- I don't do overtime.
- I am a team of one.

The Ugly

You've stumbled into a snake pit. The work may be great, the pay good, and the benefits awesome but your coworkers are vipers. This is where real stress comes from. Long hours and low wages are certainly a pain, but working with bullying, bitchiness, and harassment is toxic. Get out before you become contaminated! But first, observe and learn. You'll see nastiness and idea stealing, as well as deviousness and enough intrigue for a prime-time soap opera. You can develop strength of character that no school or loving family could ever teach you. You could absorb enough knowledge of human nature to give you the edge you need in your future work as manager, CEO, or business owner. Lucky, lucky you, to have been given this ugly experience; possibly the most valuable learning arena of your life.

To have a job you love is a wonderful thing. Work is a major chunk of your life; don't you think it should give you some pleasure? So many people live lives of "quiet desperation," afraid to make a move, afraid of the unknown. Well, paralysis isn't for you. Investigate jobs. Ask people how they make their living. Use career counselors. Read. Find out what your passion is and make that your work.

Chapter 29

Perks of the Job

And there are many! Different jobs have different payoffs. Some work is great because you're all by yourself. (If you're running a lab on the graveyard shift, you rule!) Hey, your idea of heaven could be the daily stampede at the stock exchange. Some fringe benefits are educational, some just make the job easier, and others make it fun. Some are even good for your bank account. Like, for starters, your *paycheck*! Related items are cash bonuses and company shares, although these may be down the road a bit.

Blessed are those who believe their best perk is the job itself! What does your job add to your life? Chances are there are a few goodies for you listed here:

- Paid vacation time
- Paid overtime
- Paid sick time
- Medical and/or dental plan
- Direct pay deposit
- Employee Assistance Program (EAP) for confidential help

Free Stuff

- Restaurant worker? Free food.
- Airline worker? Free (or discount) travel.
- Lab worker? Free pregnancy test.
- Retail worker? Nice discounts.

Workday Stuff

- New friends
- New romances
- Creative atmosphere
- Flex hours
- No homework!
- Challenge for your mind
- Casual dress code

Fun Stuff

Lunchtime:
- Exercise classes
- Noontime concerts
- Walks with coworkers
- Shopping

After-hours:
- Sports leagues
- Company picnics
- Christmas parties
- Fund-raisers
- Ski days
- Community participation

Educational Stuff

Use these opportunities to your benefit: Don't ever stop learning!
- Continuing education
- Lunch-and-learn seminars
- Front-row seat on office intrigue
- Free instruction in politics and bureaucracy
- Add to your résumé—experience and reference

And the best perk of your entry-level job? No place to go but up!

Part 10

You, the Student

Chapter 29

This Is *Your* Education— Go Get It!

Your school wrote and they're delighted to have you. But it'll take more than their warm welcome to put that photo of you in your cap and gown on top of your folk's TV set. Several elements will combine to get you your precious education. These include lots of cash, knowledge of the system, some loving support, and a strong focus. Take a look.

The Money Factor

An education costs a fortune and, unless there are lots of family funds floating around, paying for your schooling is going to be tough on everyone. When the parents pay the whole shot, they struggle with savings, you struggle with guilt (one hopes). Their best payback is an invitation to your graduation! If parents can't help, they get the guilt and you get student loans, with repayments till you're ninety. (Colleges and universities have lists of scholarships you may be eligible for. They're definitely worth checking out!) Most student assistance and grants, welcome as they are, barely cover tuition *and* spring break so, like most students, you'll be combining your study time with one or more paying jobs.

The best plan is to get your act together *early*. Land yourself good summer jobs, save like crazy, and pay for as much of your schooling as you can. How satisfying and motivating is that? You're financing your own path, which may differ from that of your well-meaning parents. And if you need to change your course of study, the folks may panic, but it's *your* hard-earned cash you're "being frivolous" with.

If your parents always expected you to contribute to the costs of your education, good for them. It shows the respect they have for you.

Knowing the System

There are systems in place geared solely to the well-being of students. Go check them out before your school year starts. You don't have to tell anyone that you spent a morning at the "Highlights of Note-Taking" seminar or watched the *Clueless* video (okay, actual title: *Introduction to College Life*). You have nothing to lose. If they have a "How to Not Be an Alcoholic by Christmas" presentation, could it hurt you to glance at it? Pay a little attention to the info on handling zealots and gurus who think you'd make a great addition to their cults. They're just as pushy as the beer and credit card companies—and they all want your business. You gotta be careful out there!

Child Support

If you have a family, in any form, let them rally round you while you're getting schooled. They won't always know what you need (let's face it—*you* won't always know what you need), but when you're feeling lost or lonely, family is where you can turn to. They'll forget that you haven't called in a month and that you only call when you need something. You need them now and they're there. Of course you're doing well on your own, but everyone is allowed to be needy at times. Maybe rotating sibling visits could be arranged (with care packages). Regular e-mail from the computer-savvy ones can be another comforting connection. Friends are great, but sometimes you need to pout, whine, and snivel. You're allowed, and of this you can be sure: A supportive family can take it.

The Focus Factor

What keeps you focused on your goal? An accounting student keeps a picture of the shack she grew up in as her screen saver. Her education is the ticket to her future house. Reminders of what can be done with your degree can spur you on, just as a view of the finish line is a boost to the marathon runner. So find pictures of bridges you want to build and children you want to teach and plaster them all over your walls.

Daily distractions can easily fuzz up your focus. TV, music, someone else's chewing, or a rich fantasy life can sidetrack anyone. Sometimes the most productive move is to simply give in to distractions for a short while, scream at your losing baseball team (for a few innings), then get back to molecular biology.

Give some thought to whatever juices your study style. First, you can't be cold or tired or hungry. Know your personal quirks: If silence screams at you, crank your music high. If squinting in the back booth of Sly's Bar and Grill helps you through your history exam, then make sure you tip the waiter and keep on squinting. There will be compromises to make with roommates and neighbors. You may have to move into the library. Maybe your thing is to come alive at four A.M. and hit the books then. Or not!

You've heard it before and it's a good line: *Keep your eyes on the prize!*

And now, first day of school . . . new place, new people, new level of panic. What fresh horrors await you here? Go ahead; allow yourself a few second thoughts: How will you ever fit in? Take a look around you; students are wearing their face hardware and their rainbow hair quite proudly: You'll fit fine. And how did you ever fake your way in? You earned your way in! You deserve your spot here. Relax. You've got the smarts and you can do this.

You'll soon get over the shock of finding yourself in an auditorium crowded with no one you know, facing a professor with a strange accent who lost you three statements back. Soon, anonymous faces will turn into familiar classmates, some of them close friends. You'll swap missed data and sort out the teacher's accent (Boston, USA?).

Things that keep you from your education:

- You've been deported!
- You're U2's favorite groupie, and they're touring!
- Three months of National Hockey League playoffs!
- You're the latest Hare Krishna campus recruit.
- Your contractions are three minutes apart.
- You're still quarantined with that strange rash.
- So many men, so little time!

Chapter 31

Professors, Late Papers, and Culture Shock

Here's a heads-up on the quirkiness of the keepers of your education:

- A few months into the school year you run into your anthropology prof at the hardware store. He seems strange: He's not stumbling and you can understand what he's saying; that's not strange, that's sober. Besides his drunkenness, what else have you not learned in his classroom?
- Your teacher dozes off during class questions, can't hear the question anyway, and doesn't remember the answer, well past her best-before date. Is there actually a teacher in the room?
- This class should be good: The prof has published brilliant articles and is involved with world-class research. But something is amiss. He seems annoyed that students actually show up for class. It's soon evident that he doesn't like you. He doesn't like the girl next to you either. Then everybody clues in: He hates all students! So you'll be unloved, the whole class can have a laugh over that. Just take all that he can teach you and fill in the blanks on your own.
- This teacher likes all students . . . as long as they're female. And attractive. And need their marks hiked. This prof is slime. If you need help, stick with the teaching assistant or get a tutor.
- You've scratched half a season of football viewing to concentrate on your studies. You put out some great work and you get a C? Save yourself some grief: check the buzz on which profs hand out nothing higher than Cs, and be happy with yours.

- The prof that wasn't: She's brilliant but clueless about passing her information on to the students! A walking encyclopedia that no one knows how to read. Nice if she could actually teach . . .

You'll meet them all.

This collection of symptoms is more than just quirkiness. Some professors are downright dysfunctional. You can go to your student reps for advice if your year is endangered due to bad teachers. But when you go in aware that all is not perfect in the faculty, be armed. You've come for an education; see that you get it! Access the other resources available to you.

- Teacher's assistant: If fortune is smiling upon you, your T.A. has the lowdown not only on the subject matter but also the marking scheme and the prof's idiosyncrasies. Invaluable!
- Librarians: These wonderful people are walking reference departments. They know class requirements better than you and will patiently teach you how to access them. They have set many lost students on the right path.
- Study groups: Join one or form one that matches your learning style.

- The "others": Most of your teachers do care. More than just teaching you, they want to inspire you; see the light go on in your eyes! They're not bored, or God, or drunk. (Use office hours to meet your teachers and establish a relationship with them. This time [for some students, this *is* their class time] is not only valuable for clarifications and career advice, but professors may be more inclined to forgive dedicated, hard-working students who sleep through an assignment deadline and whose laptop occasionally eats their homework . . .)

- And then there's you! Teach yourself. Stay open to how you learn best. Get some learning tools: Take any remedial writing (or reading) course given on campus. Who cares what they call it; you need it. Organize your notes, read your actual textbooks. Show up for classes. (Bonus: It's not uncommon for teachers to give up answers to upcoming tests for loyal attendees).

This you can bank on: Yes, the beginning is mind numbing, but life *will* lighten up!

Part 11

Parting Shots

Chapter 32

Reality Checks for the Newly Departed

Harsh Truths of Living on Your Own

1. There is no housecleaning fairy.
2. Your mother is no longer the alarm clock.
3. Poverty is not all it's cracked up to be.
4. The sooner your phone gets disconnected, the sooner you'll commit to your budget.
5. You are your own support system; isn't that scary?
6. Childhood is gone!

Wonders of Living on Your Own

It's your bus and you're driving it!

1. Yes, you can eat cereal for supper!
2. The mail is always for you.
3. No curfew!
4. Now you can paint your bedroom black.
5. Friends of the opposite sex can sleep over.
6. You are your own support system; isn't that great?
7. You are an adult now, a force to be reckoned with!

You know, now more than ever, how precious life is. Live yours well.

Chapter 33

Big Deal

Leaving home is a big deal. You're not just vacating the premises; you're leaving behind a lifetime of family quirks and peculiarities. No more bellowing wake-up calls; no more self-refilling fridge, and definitely no more "Where the hell have you been?" greetings to hail your three A.M. homecomings (eventually remembered as the "good old days"). Gone are the gassed-up car and the maid service. Gone too are the endless words of advice and the weekly lawn gig.

Maybe you're leaving a home where martial law ruled. Or you're digging out from under layers of smother love. Maybe you just plain don't want to go, but jobs and schools are scarce in your parts so, go you must. Yes, leaving home is a big deal.

Think of it as the ultimate adventure. Will you have a weekly crisis? No doubt. But you can handle it. Is your landlord demented? You'll win him over. Is your roommate from another planet? By next week—your new best friend.

You could get stuck with the boss without a heart, the prof without a clue. But it's true what they say: What doesn't kill you makes you stronger!

There'll be mood swings. But, from the predeparture "I'm outta here!" to the post-home-leaving "What the hell am I doing here?" know this:

- Things will get better. (Stifle that nagging thought that things couldn't possibly get worse.)

- Around you, most everyone is in the same boat, looking for a smile from someone, anyone; you can start the ball rolling.

Consider the alternative: You could go back to the parental control center, resume the battle with your siblings, have the old family curfew slapped on you, and kiss any privacy dreams good-bye. Feel better?

There'll be screw-ups: from minor ones such as the forgotten heating bills (followed by the triple-layer sweater phase) and the failed home brew experiment (although bottle caps embedded in the ceiling make an interesting decorator touch) to more serious screw-ups like throwing away your school year and getting fired yet again.

And there'll be triumphs, like coming in under budget (it may be just eight bucks but that buys you a truckload of gummy bears) or going from standing at the sink eating cold beans from the can to serving up homemade culinary masterpieces to your visiting family. How about finding a great *and* affordable place to live in, making amazing new friends, and just plain looking after yourself? You win!

You quit the home turf, adios your old friends, and shove off. Yes, you're leaving home! It's sad, exciting, scary—actually *very* scary and overwhelming. But after a while, when you've blown the grocery money and starved with your roommates, when you've negotiated a truce with your landlady over the party decibels, when you turn the key in your place and get a mini rush over the familiarity of your own little dump, you'll get it: You *are* home.

BIKES AND BABES
CHEEZO PUFFS
LYNN